The Journey from Manager to Leader:
A Playbook for Success

Published by
American Book Business Press™
http://www.american-book.com
Salt Lake City, Utah,
Printed in the United States of America on acid-free paper.

A Journal from Manager to Leader: A Playbook for Success

Designed by Stacey Poulson, design@american-book.com

Publisher's Note: *This publication is designed to provide accurate and authoritative information in regard to the subject matter covered. It is sold or distributed with the understanding that the publisher and author is not engaged in rendering legal, accounting, or other professional service. If legal advice or other expert assistance is required, the services of a competent professional person in a consultation capacity should be sought.*

Library of Congress Cataloging-in-Publication Data is available upon request.

ISBN 1-930586-65-5

Jones, William V. Jones, A Journal from Manager to Leader: A Playbook for Success

---

Special Sales

The Journey from Manager to Leader:
A Playbook for Success

William V. Jones

Dedication

To Debbie, whose support is always positive and
without reservation.

Foreword

"Leadership"—The magic elixir, the hot emphasis it gives in today's business literature, that intangible "spark" that produces quality, excellence, and high achievement. "Leadership"—the ability to pursue dreams, make things happen, get things done! "Leadership"—the ability to get people to do things they ordinarily wouldn't do and to get them to do it well! "Vision," "purposeful strategy," "empowerment," "inspiration," "teamwork," "communication," "action-enabling of others," "follower ship," "actions plans," "high quality achievement"—these are all parts of the leadership equation.

Leadership can be studied and learned in so many different ways. For the longest time, leadership was viewed as the domain of battle and sport fields. To learn leadership, we studied the great generals and ad-mirals. We studied the inspirational coaches. Our gurus became Patton and Lombardi.

Only within the last ten years has there been widespread recognition that leadership can be discerned from many other endeavors and in many different ways, in addition to the world of military and sport! Now we turn to education, to voluntary service groups, and to the world of music to see additional vivid, concrete examples of leadership.

For me personally, the American presidency has been a great leadership lab. Here we see—in ways most Americans can relate—stories of triumph and tragedy that illustrate classic leadership dos and don'ts. We have "the uppers" with the Mount Rushmore Presidents: Washington, Jefferson, Lincoln, and Teddy Roosevelt. The true heroic leaders pursuing vision, making things different and better, shifting the paradigms, and catching the new wave! Here, we also have FDR—a man confined to a wheelchair—offering the nation a sense of contagious enthusiasm and self-confidence during both the great depression and World War II. But we are also obliged to reflect on "the downers" of the nation's highest office: Wilson's frustration with the League of Nations, Hoover's inability to stop economic collapse, and the scandal and shame of "failed" presidencies.

The modern presidency affords some sophisticated insights into the leadership process. Carter, the excessive micro-manager, who needed bigger themes and a pruned agenda, who loved policy, but disdained personal politicking with Congress in support of those policies. Reagan, the consummate macro-manager, who guided with themes and slogans, loved politics but was disinclined to explore the nuts, bolts, and details of policy. (Oh, how Carter and Reagan needed a dose of each other!)

And then there were Bush, Sr. and Clinton. Bush was a remarkable wholesaler who built a historic coalition in the sand during Desert Shield and Desert Storm but who failed as a retailer, unable to relate to the worries of ordinary citizens and in the end receiving only 37 percent support in his 1992 reelection bid. There is no greater leadership paradox than William Jefferson Clinton. Talented, politically gifted, extremely bright and able, pursuing with great national support and approval a "centrist" agenda, Clinton's leadership was seriously compromised by flaws of character and human weakness. To paraphrase one of his closest aids, "Clinton was a good president who could have been a great president if he had been a better man!"

Leadership can be observed, studied, dissected, and learned from so many sources, angles, and analogies. In this book at hand, William Jones makes a major contribution to the unraveling of the leadership mystery. In this short, but most insightful leadership handbook he disseminates important leadership "golden nuggets, imaginatively imparting them with metaphors gleaned from America's favorite pastime, baseball!

Adeptly employing baseball metaphors, Jones offers many insights. Among my favorites:

- The crucial importance of orientation programs for new employees. (first inning)

- The need to profile the kinds of employees needed in the future, going far beyond mere job descriptions. (second inning)
- The imperative to understand individual as well as group needs. (third inning)
- The crucial role of positive reinforcement as an effective retention strategy. (fourth inning)
- The need to effectively develop and communicate organizational visions and a mission. (fifth inning)
- The utility of measurable outcomes in providing organizational focus and tracking organizational achievement. (sixth inning)
- How structuring the workplace as a learning environment helps counteract "the Peter Principle" of rewarding incompetence. (seventh inning)
- Develop a win-win workplace environment through teamwork and goal setting. (eighth inning)
- How stress management, adroit conflict resolution, and a healthy lifestyle are important keys to success. (ninth inning)
- Ten point plans for success and excellence. (tenth and eleventh innings)

Put these nine plus innings together with some excellent references and suggestions for further readings, and you have an "all-star" leadership manual that is guaranteed to take you to the play-offs and help you win the big game. Jones is a "big leaguer" with this book. It constitutes a "home run" contribution to leadership literature. Championship caliber; "world series" quality. Read, enjoy, and learn!!!

Dr. David C. Kozak is a professor of public policy at Gannon University in Erie, Pennsylvania, and Director of Leadership Erie. He holds a Ph.D. in public policy from the University of Pittsburgh. Previously he has served as a professor at the U.S. Air Force Academy and the National War College. He was the first recipient of the Preceptor Award given by the National Association of Community Leadership. He is a published author, national lecturer on leadership, and a frequent television commentator.

Preface

For the past thirty-five years, I have worked in a variety of environments. My first job was in fast food, which was in essence an exercise in fast service. My first boss was a short, silver-haired, intense man named Frank. Frank would watch my slower than death stride and my general "deer in headlights look" and would cluck, apparently marking time leading to his booting me out the door. Frank would hold up his index finger and thumb indicating how close I was to unemployment, then take me aside and show me the steps to speedier service. At some point, everything began to click and Frank's faith in me finally paid off. From that point forward, I acted with purpose.

My next mentor came about ten years later. During my healthcare career years, I met a physician whose knowledge, skill, and talents went beyond medicine. Dr. William Adkins was the last of the "frontiersmen" breed of individual. He did everything from big game hunting to marathon cross-country ski races. The quality that made him special was how he wanted to get everybody involved and would teach, coach, and encourage success.

Dr. Adkins was our group's "Le Director Sportif," whether it was cycling, skiing, rowing, sailing, or one of the many other athletic skills he enjoyed and promoted. If you were a novice, he would immediately begin to help you and show you how to do the activity properly and safely. He would show up at events several hours before the start to help amateur athletes with their cross-country skis, their bicycles, or other equipment that people would buy and not understand how to use it correctly. While the "weekend warriors" were prepping themselves for the event and putting a "game face" on, Dr. Adkins was working helping others and offering last minute advice. He would then go on to compete, usually finishing at or near the top.

We would all cheer our champion because he was our leader. He made these events worthwhile and turned them into learning opportunities and social happenings. At one time, Dr. Adkins' merry bunch of followers numbered nearly forty men and women trying new events and attempting to extend themselves further than they thought possible. Imagine novice cyclists riding two hundred miles in one weekend or skiing fifty kilometers in the dead of winter in the middle of Canada! These are events most people ignore or shudder to think about. But with Dr. Adkins' leadership, men and women with various degrees of skills would participate and be successful.

Dr. Adkins was special because he was a leader. He was a leader who would share his expertise without reservation with anyone. He challenged you to be better than he was. If you beat him, he was the first to congratulate your achievement. Dr. Adkins created disciples (after twenty plus years, many of us are still involved with the sports he introduced us to) not by preaching but because he cared.

The lessons I learned were to put other people first and genuinely care about their success. Further, by sharing my knowledge and skills, there was no need to worry about people abandoning me as I pushed ahead. I learned that the only power in knowledge is the gift of sharing. In today's workplace, knowledge is power only when everyone benefits. Today's hot piece of information is tomorrow's history lesson.

The ideal leader is humble. Rarely does he or she fight or push his or her way to leadership. Followers elect leaders based on the qualities they observe: the leader cares, the leader shares, and the leader will always protect those who are learning.

My philosophy will show throughout this book: teamwork, caring, sharing, and being humble. Life is too short to be controlling, deceptive, or manipulative. Corporate cultures may not endorse a political atmosphere, but it will exist. Unfortunately, too many people have not realized that positional leaders spend more time legislating and "fighting" with their employees instead of celebrating success.

I hope you find this book enjoyable to read. I know that the references, stories, and exercises will help you maintain a level of success that will create many "disciples." Like my mentor, Dr. William Adkins, I hope you can put other people first and really enjoy watching them succeed.

I will use customer service centers, sports metaphors and assorted other stories to illustrate how leadership is different from management. Many of us are managers or aspire to be a manager. A few of you will want to become leaders. To those of you that are leaders, the text of this book will seem like common sense. To those readers who choose to become leaders, you will find many valuable selections.

Table Of Contents

Coach's Chalkboard
Need for Talent
Warming Up
Success
Reduce the Insanity
Fantasy Leagues
Observation
Visualization
Controlling Stress
Quick Decisions
Retaining Talented People
Treat Employees as Customers
Shortsightedness
Web Sites That Promote Leadership
Winners and Losers
Undermining
Employees' Perception of Work
Meaningful Work
Timing Is Critical for Success

Warming Up

Creating a winning team begins with understanding the skill positions. If you were the coach for a baseball team, would you put a slow, less mobile person at shortstop or first base? Perhaps you might use that player as a temporary solution, but for the long term you will seek a player that fits the profile for that position.

As a coach, if you do not know immediately what skills are needed for each position, you quickly learn by profiling championship teams or individuals. As a country, China was never known for its ability to produce Olympic level divers. Chinese coaches studied films of the great American diver, Greg Louganis, and constructed a frame-by-frame profile of every dive he performed as a champion. The coaches then instructed their students on the techniques, practicing the captured images countless times and perfecting every movement.

Today, Chinese divers are some of the best divers in Olympic competition.

As a manager, have you profiled your best employees? If you tell someone that a certain man or woman is the best salesperson in your organization, can you detail why? Are you basing your opinion on accumulated quantifiable information from phone or sales statistics, customer satisfaction, or some combination of measurement? Once you have found your best, what education are you providing others to create more people with the same excellence? In your opinion, do you think the Chinese have stopped profiling their champions and will leave the next generation of competitors to excel through chance?

Top Of The First

Julianne read the newspaper ad with great interest. "Work for a progressive, rapidly expanding company offering on the job training, competitive wages, and benefits. No experience necessary. Our customer service organization will train you to be a successful company representative. Join the future now and be trained in this rapidly expanding field. Call today!"

Julianne could not believe job opportunities like this existed. Grandpa always said that "if it looks too good to be true, it's probably too good to be true." However, this was a major company right in her hometown. It had millions of customers and was successful. Why, even Helen down the street is now working there and Julianne thought that she would be a better worker than Helen could ever hope to be. Grandpa was wrong and the ad had to be true.

Julianne was a high school graduate and mother of three almost grown children. She was a single mom because an accident killed her husband, Tim, a couple of years ago. The insurance money took care of many family needs and Julianne worked at a variety of part-time jobs. She felt these combined experiences would prepare her for the next step to full-time employment for a major company.

The ad didn't say anything about computer experience, only that training would be available. Julianne knew nothing about computers. She had taken some typing classes in high school years ago. While the kids wanted a computer, "adult stuff" concerned Julianne so she told them they received enough computer training at school. She didn't like the idea of the World Wide Web. Tomorrow, she would go to the recruiting office and fill out an application.

The recruiting office bustled with activity by office people scurrying back and forth. Important looking people with suit and ties were looking at bulletin boards filled with information. Other potential new employees were sitting with clipboards quickly writing as though taking a timed test. Julianne was glad she had worn a business outfit. Finally, she caught the attention of a busy girl behind a desk.

"Here for a job?" asked the receptionist.

"Yes, I am." Julianne wanted to sound confident.

"Here's a clipboard and the application. Fill it out and be complete. If it's not complete we can't see you." The girl acted like she said the same thing to people a hundred times a day. The girl reminded Julianne of the cashiers at stores, who say, "Have a nice day" a hundred times, never meaning it.

Julianne took the clipboard and looked for a place to sit. On a loveseat sat two kids filling out applications, no room there. On a couch (strange furniture for such a huge company, she thought) sat two men. Not there. Finally, a person stopped writing, and offered Julianne her chair.

"Thank you. It's really busy and there aren't many places to sit," Julianne said.

Julianne's turn to meet with one of the office people was coming next. Working behind one of the desks she saw a familiar face in Brad. She hoped to see Brad, a kid her son knew in high school who had been over to her house for several meals. Brad would make her feel more comfortable. From behind came a voice, "Where's Julianne?" someone asked in kind of slurred pronunciation.

"Oh, that's me." (Taken off-guard, Julianne nearly dropped her coat and purse on the floor. Not a good impression!)

At the same time, Brad spoke, "If you don't mind, Jake, I'll take care of Mrs. Muncie." Relieved, Julianne thanked Jake and said she would wait.

Brad was sharply dressed, almost to the point that he should be an executive. He apologized for the environment and the way people are treated in general.

"People are coming out of the woodwork, Mrs. Muncie! We get overwhelmed sometimes."

Julianne, wanting everything to go well, told Brad not to worry; it was okay for him to call her Julianne. This was Brad's first job out of high school and he was diligent.

"You know, Mrs. Muncie, the company is growing so fast, that with any luck I think I can be in middle management in a couple of years."

"That's wonderful, Brad. I hope you make your goals."

"Now, what can I do for you today?"

Julianne explained she was applying for a job at the customer service center.

"Well, Mrs. Muncie, everybody gets a job here and the training is pretty good. I never heard about anybody getting fired because they couldn't do the job." Wow, what a relief those words were to Julianne!

"You'll pick up everything and learn your job faster than you thought possible. It's not easy, but nobody seems to have any problems."

At some point, Julianne stopped listening to Brad once she realized her fears were not going to come true. The application process was over and the next step would be the interview. Brad assured Julianne the job was hers and the interview was just a formality.

"The company is desperate. They're taking everybody who is breathing. If you don't say anything stupid, you'll get the job."

Julianne appreciated Brad's openness to a degree. However, she felt a little insulted that everybody who can breathe gets hired. The "stupid" comment also concerned her. The interview would be in two days. Julianne went home.

The events surrounding the interview were bizarre. The directions sent Julianne to a building on the West Side of town. She finally found the right building after searching the mismarked industrial park. Parking was tight and she hoped she hadn't taken somebody's spot, especially somebody important.

She went inside and was stunned. The world she saw was unbelievable. A sea of cubicles and people were everywhere. It was a huge warehouse with no windows and big ceiling fans circulating the inside air.

Julianne stood and watched for several minutes. Once in a while a person would "pop up" and hurry to another desk, talk to someone, then hurry back to his or her cubicle. Then another person would pop up; then someone would yell something across several rows. Julianne thought it was like something she saw in a prairie dog nature show. Little heads popping out of holes, looking around, and then disappearing back into the holes again.

The endless activity created a chaotic atmosphere. Julianne felt concern building in her stomach and started questioning her presence. She started to doubt if she could work in this environment and do this job.

"Do you need help?" The question snapped Julianne out of her thoughts. She turned around and smiled at the man with a big coffee cup.

"Yes, I'm here for an interview."

"Do you know who you are supposed to see? Three departments are located here and different people do the interviews. What job did you apply for?" He spoke quickly and Julianne had to focus on his words.

"Just a call center job." Julianne wasn't quite sure what she and Brad had talked about. Panic started to build because she felt vulnerable.

"Hang on and I'll find out. What's your name?"

"Julianne Muncie."

"Okay. Just a minute. You know recruiting should at least give people a name before they send folks over for interviews. At least you wouldn't feel so lost."

Pretty soon, the big coffee cup guy came back with another guy. "Julianne, this is Dick. He'll be doing your interview."

"Yeah, I wasn't expecting you until eleven or so." Dick seemed nice, albeit a quiet type.

"I got here early because I wasn't sure where to go. I'm sorry."

Dick cleared his throat, probably out of necessity from the years of cigarette smoking. "I'm going to have you sit in our break room until I get a couple of things done." Big coffee cup guy disappeared into the sea of cubicles.

Dick led Julianne to the break room. "Help yourself to some coffee. I'll be right back."

Julianne sat and looked over at the coffeepot sitting on the burner. Julianne could see the pot was almost empty and smelled a little burned. Dick would only be a couple of minutes, so she passed on the coffee idea.

An hour passed before Dick returned. He cleared his throat, and then continued, "I'm sorry. I got sidetracked and forgot you were waiting for me. I'd lose my head if it weren't attached!"

"That's okay. I understand." Julianne didn't understand but it seemed appropriate to say.

Julianne felt uncomfortable throughout her meeting with Dick. He kept clearing his throat and talking in low volume. He constantly fumbled through papers, scratched his head and occasionally mumbled. Dick asked what kind of computer experience she had.

"None. I don't even own a computer."

Dick replied, clearing his throat, "Well, don't worry. That's why we got trainers. You'll get it. Everybody else does. You ever think to take some computer classes? It is a high-tech kind of world now?"

Julianne thought computers would make the job easier. She thought that's why they're everywhere. How hard could computers be? She had seen kids play games on them and they seemed to be having fun.

The interview was over in fifteen minutes. Dick had other people to see and needed to make up the hour because he was behind. Julianne answered a few questions and felt okay about her answers. It was obvious Dick did a lot of interviews, which made him a hard read. Julianne left the building thinking this is what big companies are all about.

One week later, Julianne got a job-offer letter in the mail. She was going start in two weeks as a service representative. An orientation program started that day at a nearby building.

The orientation program was held in a small room with computers and desks. Julianne got the last chair. Due to a parking shortage, she arrived several minutes late.

"That computer doesn't work," whispered the girl next to her. Great, thought Julianne. I'm the one with the least experience in the room and the only one with a broken computer.

The trainer gave a program overview. She was not sure everyone would be ready with such an aggressive timetable. But the boss wanted people on the floor ASAP and thorough training would just have to wait until later. The scaled-back program included two products, their service related issues, and the five software programs that support the products.

Julianne was mortified! Multiple software programs plus Windows and the Internet! There was no way she could be ready.

The first day ended and Julianne was exhausted. The instructor's lectures went on and on. Julianne thought she'd be lucky to remember half of what was said that day. The broken computer didn't matter because the instructor never even had them turn on the darn contraption. All she did was say what programs would be easy to learn and which ones would take months to learn. Months! How would she ever be able to help a customer when it takes months to learn the software? She was sure she was going to fail.

Each day the instructor droned on about the products, assignments, rules and procedures, and software. It was the end of the first week and no one had seen the software. Two weeks to go for something that takes six months to learn.

The second week started with "side-jacking," a term used to describe sitting with an experienced partner. The trainer told Julianne to sit with Karrie, a bubbly twenty-something who bounced around like a super ball! Karrie had been with the company for three months. Julianne was impressed. "Wow, you got all this down pat in three months and now you are teaching me!"

"Don't kid yourself. I hardly know what I'm doing. I just ask the people around me when I need help and try to remember how to do the same process again for the next customer," Karrie said.

"Aren't you concerned about helping customers who call in?" Julianne asked.

"Most people are as lost as we are about all this technology. We just give them a standard response and ask them to wait to see if the problem clears up and if not, call us back tomorrow. The problem is that there are so many situations we are not prepared for so we make things up or send it to a supervisor. We all try to do our best but there is just too much to remember."

Julianne was taken aback. She had a work ethic and this behavior seemed odd. She always tried to instill in her children the idea of hard work and dedication. But how could she meet her own standards of excellence with so much unknown? Julianne wondered how a company could be successful with what she perceived as chaos and poor planning?

Karrie got a call from a customer asking about their long distance service. "It looks like you are active with us, what's your question? Did you call the toll-free number to see who your long distance carrier is? Sometimes people don't get our service right away because they have a "freeze" on their line. Call your local company and they'll fix it for you. They said to call here; well they were wrong. You need to call them. No, I can't help you any further. Well, it's company policy for us not to get involved if you have a freeze on your line. Okay, is there anything else I can help you with today? Okay, bye-bye."

The customer hardly spoke. Karrie jumped to the conclusion that the local telephone company or the customer was at fault. Julianne wondered how Karrie could be considered an appropriate role model? Were these the behaviors and responses the company wanted her to acquire?

"Karrie, I can't believe you would talk to customers that way. Aren't you concerned someone will overhear you?"

"No. The people who listen in to grade our calls are our friends and score us high. Plus, I was right and the customer was stupid. He should've removed the freeze on his phone and everything would've gone through without a hitch."

So it went for the entire day. Karrie spent as much time wandering around looking for help as she did on the phone. Occasionally, she would shine and show some expertise; however, most of the time, she did her nails, looked upset whenever a call came her way, and ended calls abruptly. Karrie explained the computer systems are lousy and take way too long to get you the customer or for you to do the necessary documentation. Furthermore, she felt much of the documentation was busywork. She had little respect for the team leaders or supervisors. "They don't know anything about our jobs."

The next day, Julianne sat in class thinking about Karrie's attitude. My gosh, she has only been here several months and she is already acting with indifference! Julianne wondered if this was her fate.

Actually, her perceived fate may have been better than what did happen. Computer software training started. The instructor blitzed through the first screens. She used terms like "backspace," "enter," "spacebar," and so forth. Julianne asked John what to do next. He seemed okay with the questions because the class was going too slow for his liking. It kept him busy and helped him pass the time. He didn't teach her anything. He would just point to the keyboard or the monitor. Sometimes he would just take over and do it quickly himself. Julianne was caught up with the rest of the group, but had no idea how.

Julianne spent the next few days listening to Karrie. The act was getting old, plus Julianne's agenda was to learn. Karrie went too fast and kept saying she wasn't comfortable showing her anything because she wasn't sure if she was right. Also, she said, "several people let the 'guys' know that if they wanted floor training to continue, they wanted a raise. Well, nothing had been done about the request at this time, so everybody was refusing to show the new people much."

At the end of the second week, Julianne was ready to quit. She felt extremely frustrated and demoralized.

"Julianne, don't quit. I think you can get this stuff and you'll be good at this job. Everybody feels this way during training. Then you go out to the floor and people support you and you keep learning in leaps and bounds. Give it some more time," the instructor said convincingly.

Julianne did her best to learn the software. She would learn pieces of the routine, but then another product would come up and she would forget what to do. She knew she wasn't always listening to the customer. She was too concerned about the software.

The class "graduated" and was assigned to a shift with a person from the group who was supposed to be his or her mentor. Julianne and John (the computer whiz) were on the same shift (Karrie fortunately was on another shift). Even though John was sharp, he didn't have much skill on the phones. He would mumble and customers didn't understand him. Julianne realized right away that she should leave him alone. Instead she thought she could use the team leaders.

Wow, what an eye opener. They seemed bothered by Julianne's questions. They kept saying how useless the trainers were and why bother training people if this was the best that could be done. The manager asked Julianne if she could at least say hello over the phone. The manager had too much to do to baby-sit Julianne. She suggested she refer to her materials to learn what to do. "This job needs people who can think on their own."

This constant struggle continued for another month. Every afternoon, Julianne could feel herself getting sick thinking about the calls she would have to take and the general lack of support. Overall, the job was too stressful. Her kids kept telling her to quit. Julianne hated the thought of being a quitter.

The other people had no intention of quitting. They needed the job and the benefits to support their families. Their attitude was if the bosses don't care what's going on, why should they care?

Brad was right: no one lost his or her job. The company kept hiring more people. Julianne moved to a day shift because the new people were taking over her shift. People joked that she could be a team leader in a couple of months. Julianne chuckled; she was so poorly prepared for her job that she never earned a bonus check for any of the measurements that management tracked.

Julianne needed to quit. The fact that she could not master the software bothered her. When she tried to be thorough in her assistance, the supervisors would tell her she spent too much time on the call. Occasionally, irate customers would call, cursing and screaming at her like she had caused the problem. Everything was swirling around in her head: no support, poor training, supervisors who didn't seem to care, people with no dedication to their job, and monitored breaks, like she was in kindergarten. The lack of trust upset Julianne.

She finally quit. Julianne went back to working part-time jobs. She was sleeping again every night like she used to sleep. She was amazed she was able to last as long as she did. She hated the thought that she wanted to quit!

Julianne stayed in touch with some of her friends at the call center. They talk about all the new rules, who is getting promoted, and the people that left for other jobs. Her friends said she had courage to quit. Julianne knew her decision to give up the money and benefits was difficult, but the work was too stressful and there was other available employment.

Julianne still didn't know computers; other people would help complete her work. She started to laugh when she thought about how many times she had been written up for not knowing what to do. They were even going to put her in the team performance improvement program. More useless training in Julianne's opinion since it didn't address her real needs. She wasn't taught properly from the start; so all the corrective training in the world wouldn't make a difference.

Julianne would never know if she could reach her potential. She never had a chance and no one seemed to care. Long ago, her interviewer Dick had stated, "everybody is expendable." His job was to put round pegs in square holes. If the peg became misshapen while trimming, he would just go back to the barrel and get another peg.

COACH'S CHALKBOARD

Success is a learned behavior modeled by successful people. In sports, championship teams talk about the importance of "clubhouse leadership." Teams will acquire seasoned veterans for a championship run because of their past experiences with winning organizations. The team is seeking successful modeling to show other players what it takes to achieve excellence.

During a recent baseball season, the Houston Astros were picked by many analysts to repeat as divisional champs and possibly contend for the World Series title. During the off-season, several veterans were traded to reduce the team's commitment to salaries and occasionally because a player was thought to be "done." But these players offered more than everyday baseball contributions; they modeled leadership. The team suffered a horrible season and at one point had the worst record in baseball. The clubhouse leadership was missing and the proud organization tumbled mightily. The baseball club the veterans were traded to did make the play-offs that year.

Simulation training can properly prepare new employees for the rigors of the job by modeling desired behaviors. Unfortunately, to create simulations takes time, money, and a talented educational team. If education is not strategically linked to the organization's mission and vision, it is unlikely that the company will commit resources to create this kind of learning environment. Companies that use simulation exercises to prepare persons for the work environment are difficult to find. It is ironic that when an employee gets stuck, his or her first move is to ask their neighbor how to accomplish the task. The neighbor shows them how it's done; the employee logs the sequence and the result. If the result is successful (positive customer feedback), the event is internalized and practiced again in the future.

As you continue reading, think about Julianne and how the company introduced her into the customer service world.

How do you create more empathy, better preparation, and support?

What do you think about caring, leadership, and retention of employees?

Pick a process you think is necessary for success in the workplace. How do you prepare a simulation exercise to model essential behaviors?

BACKGROUND

Recruiting and hiring employees is like bargain shopping: companies are seeking people with high quality for a low price. This is becoming a difficult task as the labor pool continues to shrink.

Look at the following recent job data from the U.S. Department of Labor to understand how difficult it is to recruit employees in general:

1. Between September and October 1999, the number of unemployed people declined by 70,000 and the number of retiring persons was 58,000;
2. In the same period, the unemployment rate was 4.1%; and,
3. Non-retail services added 215,000 workers during October.

Over 70,000 customer service centers are operating in the United States, creating fierce competition for the small number of available people who meet two criteria:

1. A good job match and
2. Long-term loyalty.

The customer service center employee is the companies' frontline representative to the customer. If company contact is to represent a true competitive advantage over similar companies in the industry, choosing people carefully is paramount. Also, placing a person in a work environment geared for learning, success, and compensation is also important.

It appears many companies "over hire" in an attempt to locate quality persons. Unfortunately, this strategy stresses a company's limited resources, particularly for education and training. The most frequent result with over hiring is it reduces the opportunity to capture any return on investment, currently estimated at six to twelve months of continued employment.

Management literature suggests that:
- Dissatisfied employees are less productive,
- Share their dissatisfaction with customers,
- Work at a far less productivity level than their counterparts and,
- Feel that their managers are powerless to motivate them.

Managers, held accountable for the outcomes in their work environment, feel the pressures of these negative attitudes and consequences. Providing quality leadership, innovative work environment ideas, and a commitment to excellence seems unlikely when people struggle in day-to-day survival.

Managers typically run the work environment by creating a status quo. Leadership challenges the status quo and asks the manager to become a catalyst for excellence and quality outcomes. A comical definition of insanity suggests it is the result of doing the same thing over and over again expecting different results. Managers are sacrificed when profits go sour (over a million managers lost their jobs in the early 1990s). Knowing that you might be the scapegoat for an organization's downturn, why not challenge the system and create a workplace that seeks excellence by creating a learning environment for the employees? Why not create a workplace with caring, emotionally charged individuals working together to create a winning team? Will it hurt productivity to make the workplace more fun?

Today's customer already has high expectations about a product's features and benefits. The intangibles they seek that will allow companies to prosper are:

1. How well the employee gives meaningful advice about the product or the reason for the call and,
2. The amount of interaction with the customer service representative that yields new learning or information.

Work environments need employees coached to see excellence as the norm. To reach this goal, the following steps need to be taken:

1. Recruit talented individuals with the majority of the skills and knowledge the job requires,
2. Have managers who embrace leadership and,
3. Provide simulation education that creates properly prepared employees who can problem solve.

Many people own dogs and have to deal with the summer flea infestation. Dog owners realize it is not enough to have the dog groomed and dipped in flea treatments. The owner needs to bomb the house with aerosols to kill the fleas and their eggs in the carpet, furniture, and curtains. Otherwise, the family pet only experiences momentary relief and the fleas attack again when the dog returns.

Workplace changes are like the family pet's fight with fleas. When recruiting brings in talented people and the educator prepares them for success, these efforts will be sabotaged if the management team and the coworkers don't support excellence. The new people will adopt the position of mediocrity.

Leadership

Leadership is not about cheerleading. Leadership is about creating focus through measurable objectives designed to help each person to reach success. Leadership is about listening, inspiring trust, and fostering a commitment to the workplace. Leadership is about helping others exert their influence on achieving excellence and creating a sense of community among employees. A leader takes responsibility for failure and lets others claim success. People who follow a leader do so without legislation. Leaders provide confidence to seek future challenges.

Leaders are challenged by the demands of the organization's mission to achieve meaningful outcomes. If managers focus on outcomes and not the process, success will be intermittent and hard to replicate. Leaders understand that people don't fail; it is the process that fails people. It is imperative for leaders to simplify the complex.

Demographic data suggests that the people available for employment will be at a disadvantage, be it from lack of education or experiences in the workplace. Many people that will be hired have never worked in a "melting pot" of cultural diversity. The manager as a leader will take advantage of the different age and sex groups and the various cultural backgrounds to form a championship team.

Despite naysayers, it is not impossible to create a diversified workforce. Take a look at the rosters of baseball, soccer, or hockey teams. These teams all have players from different countries, different languages, and different customs. Yet, championship teams are comprised of this "melting pot" because each player knows his or her role and contributes to excellence. Language is not a barrier when the process is clearly defined. Excellence is a result of simplified processes, not a focus on the outcomes. Vince Lombardi is famous for having said, "Practice does not make perfect. Perfect practice makes perfect."

Anybody can lead or manage when times are good and companies are profitable. The true leaders come forth when the times are tough.

COACH'S CHALKBOARD

Every environment is a reflection of the leader's knowledge, attitude, and behavior. Moral standards, importance of family and friendship, support, and even humor develop from the persons perceived by the workforce as "in charge."

In the 1994 AFC Championship game, the Pittsburgh Steelers had the ball on the San Diego three-yard line with time running out. It was going to be a fourth-down play to either win and move on to the Super Bowl or lose and go home. The Pittsburgh quarterback, Neil O'Donnell, called a timeout to talk strategy with head coach, Bill Cowher, a highly stressful moment as many players wondered which play would be called to win the game. Most viewers probably expected to see Cowher and his coaching staff looking worried with penetrating eyes and stiff lips.

Instead, Cowher was smiling and he was relaxed and confident. He brought his quarterback over to the sideline to help him relax and be confident. It was an amazing scene—a coach in the middle of a crisis with a big smile on his face and welcoming his quarterback with schoolboy enthusiasm. There should be a happy ending, but the perfect play was thwarted by a spectacular play by a San Diego linebacker who managed to tip the pass at the last second and preserve the victory.

Nonetheless, that moment defined the attitude and character of the next three seasons as the Steelers went to Super Bowl XXX and another AFC Championship game in 1997. Those four highly successful years defined the team as a reflection of their coach: determined to win and working together as a team.

This is the lesson for customer service centers: the job is important and essential for companies in this highly competitive environment. But, it is not brain surgery and certainly mistakes are not going to result in life or death scenarios. Leaders need to be humanistic and get the most out of the workforce through empathy and humor.

Top Of The Second

COACH'S CHALKBOARD
To reduce the insanity, try the following steps:
1. Start with talented individuals,
2. Create a learning environment,
3. Establish quality outcomes,
4. Develop mentors and coaches,
5. Provide the tools and information needed to complete tasks and,
6. Develop career paths to maintain employee loyalty.

Profiling
Recruiters in sport programs demonstrate how effective profiling can be for reaching goals. If a school or team is recruiting a football player, a player must meet certain criteria before coaches will arrange an interview. Physical size, demonstrable physical skills, and intangibles such as attitude and leadership are reviewed

about each candidate. Many times, teams don't fill a position but take the best athletes available to help the team. Knowledge and skills can be taught; leadership, attitude, and quick assimilation are inherited talents. In the sports world, the difference between championships and last place may be one or two athletes.

The workplace is not much different: one or two quality workers can have a championship impact for the overall organization. Focusing on the best will yield measurable excellence. Those employees who demonstrate mediocrity (or less) need coaching and leadership from those who excel. Either coach people to make them better with your customers or have them support the organization in a different capacity. Managers and employees cannot always be right when selecting jobs in the workplace. It is not a mistake to admit a mismatch has occurred; it is a mistake to continue trying to make it work. How many times in sports do you read about an athlete who was moved to a different position and blossomed into a star? This is what leaders and managers do: they help people become successful. If you don't make these subtle changes in the workplace, poorly matched employees will fail to contribute adequately and will hurt the overall outcomes.

Many companies recruit for an open position instead of recruiting for the best talent available. Talented people who have some of the knowledge and skills needed for the job will perform better than a person with equal knowledge and skills but with no talent for the job. Knowing whom to hire begins by profiling the best performers working in the customer service center. Knowledge and skills are improved through simulation training and "just in time" support (electronic or classroom help). So, what talents are necessary to complete the position?

Talents are non-trainable attributes like personality, creativity, and problem solving. A master chef can mix exotic ingredients to make outstanding soup. Talented employees can mix intangibles with knowledge to address customer needs. This recipe creates a higher degree of loyalty for both the customer and the employee. Both persons will stay with the company longer.

A talented employee allows a manager to measure quality outcomes. The employee sounds confident and competent resulting in higher customer confidence. If the customer perceives quality, customer satisfaction rises. The true measure of quality outcomes is what the customer thinks of the service and how they present those impressions to others.

Recruiting is responsible for finding new employees. A recruiter needs to know the profile necessary to match the person to the job. If the manager cannot profile the person based on the best performers, recruiting will supply the wrong people. If the manager does not have a plan with measurable outcomes for the recruiter to use for matching people and jobs, again, they will select the wrong people. If a manager wants to change the hiring results, he or she needs to be active in the recruiting process. The recruiter and manager need to work as a team long before the interview process begins.

COACH'S CHALKBOARD

To gain a better understanding of profiling and assembling a championship team, join a fantasy league (baseball, basketball, or football, for example). Using the Internet, initiate your search with a search engine like www.yahoo.com to locate free fantasy leagues. As an "owner," you will be given a budget and a selection of players to track throughout the season. You will be able to make trades or seek other players to add to your roster (depending on the rules of the league). You will track performances on-line using the statistics compiled by the league. It is a great way to learn how to manage skill positions to maximize benefits to the team.

Orientation

Once recruiting has been completed, it is time to bring people in for an orientation program. Orientation begins with everyone new to the company. It is one of the few times people from various departments are gathered together in large companies. What an opportunity to lead the group through team-building exercises! It is easier to get a person from the finance department to help out a person from the customer service center if the two people know each other.

Both the company and the new employee sometimes discount the importance of the orientation program. Companies may have a formal program and in many cases this includes benefits and information culled from the current employee handbook. The program will run the gambit from dry to lively and may include a litany of "guest speakers" to review essential information, particularly how a person may lose their job (time card abuse, tardiness, and sexual harassment, for example).

Consider a paradigm shift and make orientation the kickoff to quality employee involvement. For example, in colleges and universities, the orientation week is a celebration and a collection of activities designed to introduce incoming student to campus life. Loyalty to the university begins during this week as students are given mentors, introduced to people with similar interests, and immersed in the sights and sounds of higher education. The school provides tours, refreshments with the faculty, concerts and dances, and special luncheons and dinners. The school introduces procedures and rules by using mentors as part of the socialization activities, just talk between new friends.

Students are immediately absorbed into the college culture. They shed their high school colors and adopt the new school's colors and mascots. The students go from "deer in the headlights" looks to a swagger that says they are college students. Few freshmen feel the need to return home to see mom and dad anytime soon. They hardly resemble the sad boy or girl the parents left behind just days before.

Consider your company's history and image during orientation program. For example, colleges prepare trophy rooms to share the success of their athletic and sports fetes. Where is your trophy room? Surely community groups have presented plaques and recognition for the service provided by the company to the community!

At college, key buildings are made the centerpiece of campus with hallways lined with pictures of past presidents and successful alumni. Parents are paraded through these hallways to inspire dreams of success and wealth for their children. The buildings literally drip with history and achievement. People stand in awe of the rich tradition. Have you ever been in the offices of someone like Joe Paterno (Penn State) or Tubby Raymond (Delaware)? Competition for quality athletes is intense and giving athletes tours of key offices lined with trophies, successful athletes, and other memorabilia makes the young athlete's eyes swell with desire to join the organization. In your opinion, do you think top high school athletes will be impressed with their dorm room or the study cubicle in the library? The only organization that makes a Spartan lifestyle part of its heritage and recruiting is the U.S. Marine Corps.

Why would new employees see the orientation program as a day away from the new job and a few hours away from their work cubicle? Perhaps they go because of the lure of free coffee and donuts to help ease the blasé dissemination of information? Should not orientation be a celebration of the company's growth? What about a goal that everyone meets five new people and agrees to keep in touch with them at least once a month?

Orientation is an opportunity to build pride and a sense of belonging and caring in new employees. Team building activities that stress teamwork, communication skills, fun, and a sense of accomplishment are ideal for generating camaraderie among new people. Inviting top echelon managers to share refreshments and meet new people gives life to commitment. What a thrill for a new employee to shake the hand of his or her CEO! And, why not a picture of the CEO and of each team from the team-building activities that will be framed and given to each employee for his or her desk? A gentle reminder for the new person that when times are tough there is a team of people he or she can call.

Education

When considering results, think about how a slinky works. You pick it up and stretch it out but its natural tendency is to return to the middle. If the slinky is not overly stressed, it will stretch and return to the center again. When the slinky is pulled apart, the greatest energy potential now exists. The slinky can take on a life of its own.

People are much like a slinky. A heterogeneous group of new employees will posses a variety of skills, knowledge and talents that will stretch from high to low. Educators will focus materials and effort between the best and the worst. Because resources are limited, the top learners are given less attention and instead encouraged to self-instruction. Without the proper motivation, top performers tend to lose motivation and drift back to the center. Focusing on the wrong end (even the middle) will yield a class of mediocre performers. The stretched slinky created the most potential for energizing the learning environment but, the top performers were not singled out to lead in a more challenging environment.

It is not suggested people are lazy and lack self-motivation. People respond to their environment and they will seek a comfort zone to minimize stress. Product and software knowledge and skills can dominate employee training. Ultimately, training will focus on the employee by repeating product features such as warranties and company policies while banging away on their keyboard. Soft skills such as listening, conversational customer needs analysis and open-ended problem solving are offered as a sidebar with minimal practice time.

Too many of today's representatives say things like "It's company policy" or "I'm not allowed to do that" or "I can't help you." These phrases are the result of knowledge and skill training emphasizing a limited course of action. Training also creates dependency on management for creative problem solving, leading to less efficiency, and less customer satisfaction. Skills and knowledge are important only as a foundation. Classroom time is best spent creating thinkers, detectives, advisors, mentors, coaches, and future educators.

Learning in adult education is rarely a linear event. Everyone has some history that lends itself to certain knowledge, skills, and talent. It is insulting to the learner for the educator to provide the same training to everyone. The new century's classroom is comprised of menus, designed to provide "just in time" segmented learning that the students picks to begin. Remember, the outcome is to meet the profile and objectives of the workplace's best personnel. How students get there is their choice.

Adult learning is more than the distribution of information and skills. It is about profiles that identify what is known and what is needed, otherwise called "gap analysis." An educator who understands needs will keep the "slinky" energized by delivering material that challenges the top performers and appropriately leads the learners with significant gaps.

The classroom becomes a "supermarket" where learners are free to choose the learning products that reduce the gap. The products are simulation exercises based on the actual experiences culled from top performers in the organization. The computer becomes the individual's coach, allowing the learner to try as many attempts as necessary to reach successful completion of the simulation. The human instructor is free to roam the room to offer challenges, coach possible solutions to unusual circumstances, and to offer encouragement to those who are struggling.

Simulation training is not lectures and visual aids reformatted into a computer. The training is interactive based on storyboards constructed from actual experiences. When constructed properly, the learner makes choices based on the information presented in the scenario. As levels of difficulty increase, the choices become less obvious and solutions become less right versus wrong. Failure is a distinct possibility because it challenges the learner to think and retry in order to go on to the next level. Just like a video game, every level becomes more challenging and begins to consume the learner. Learning is now emotional as the person is driven to get to the next level.

This type of classroom is not easy to construct and not many company educators understand how to build this type of learning environment. To begin the process, hire outside consultants who specialize in adult learning psychology, instructional design and computer programming to develop your initial programs. The outcome will be a sophisticated methodology that can be measured and replicated in each learner. Simulation training must work if you consider the outcomes displayed by pilots in the Gulf War, the success of the space program and the ability of airline pilots to avoid in-flight disasters.

Managers should make the assumption that today's jobs are more complex than the ones people had twenty years ago. Interactions with customers are difficult and much is expected.

Using the Internet to support a company's growth will be integral over the next five years. Interactive Web sites allow customers to connect with a "live" person almost immediately and will be viewed as essential with quality as the norm. Companies will be spending a great amount of resources developing phone consultants for their interactive sites.

Companies use customer service centers as their visible commitment to quality. They will even chant quotes like "the customer is number one." Yet too many times, the workplace objectives are answer the phone quickly, keep call abandonment to the minimum, and stay on the phone ready for the next call. The company offers bonuses for the manager's ability to meet these quantifiable objectives. It is important to recall a philosophy that suggests managers treat their employees as they want the employees to treat the company's customers. Employee retention will be the manager's greatest challenge. Less than 10 percent employee turnover will be the operating standard. The employee is number one because he or she takes care of the company's customers.

Here is a simple test to learn if managers and others responsible for employee development grasp the importance of knowing customers. Once a week, have managers write three things they learned from customers and three things they learned from employees. If the manager can list six or more things they learned per week, they are listening to the workforce and the customer. What mangers learn each week will become the scripts for future simulation training events.

COACH'S CHALKBOARD

Many authorities consider Leonardo Da Vinci the greatest creative thinker of all time. Da Vinci addressed everything from flying machines to medicine. What was the source for his inspiration? Nature, the environment, and people gave Da Vinci his creative genius. His "super human" power was based on observation and his ability to keep extensive notes on everything he observed. His notebooks are filled with observations, drawings, and new thinking.

In the movie, *Indiana Jones and the Last Crusade,* the item of supreme importance was the notebook belonging to the elder Dr. Jones (Sean Connery). The majority of the movie was devoted to the loss and retrieval of the notebook. The book contained necessary information on recovering precious artifacts from the Crusades. Without the book, the exact location of the artifacts was unknown and the many traps were impossible to navigate. This book was so valuable that everywhere it went, death and mayhem followed. Dr. Jones studied the Crusades, understood the secrets, and wrote his knowledge in the book.

In medicine, physicians making rounds in teaching hospitals also use notebooks (albeit note cards held together with rubber bands) to review patient histories and create new thinking. As much as people want to think that medicine is a science, it as much an art today as it was one hundred years ago. Therefore, it becomes necessary for a doctor to remember his or her patient, the medical tests and results, and the previous strategies in order to try to help the person make progress. These notes are meticulously updated and become the source of new and important knowledge.

As a manager and a leader, what note cards are you carrying? Do you have file folders on individuals that may eventually justify no raise or termination, or folders that detail a person's contributions, their objectives, and measured improvements? Are your notes and folders used for defense of an annual review or cause for celebration? Your observations will influence the workplace and help determine future growth. Are you adding to the bottom line by observing the environment and learning?

The point of contact is the employee with the customer. Preparing the employee with knowledge and little else will create a consultant who will react in the following ways:

1. Defensive posture by talking over the customer's head,
2. Defensive posture by patronizing the customer, or
3. Defensive posture by hiding behind "company policy."

An employee who adopts knowledge and skill sets and implements them efficiently will have outstanding quantitative numbers. This person will answer many calls on a daily basis; they will have high occupancy time, and will contribute to a lower abandonment rate. For many managers, the efficient person is the handle for the next rung on the ladder. In the customer's eyes, it could be another frustrating attempt to have their needs addressed.

Part of the solution of a new orientation and training model is to simplify. Create easily learned administrative systems. Reduce the rules and procedures that add little to productivity and quality outcomes. Just because technology exists to monitor every minute an employee spends on the job, is it necessary? This monitoring has no relationship with quality outcomes. It gives people the impression they cannot be trusted to do their work without a "big brother" watching. It makes more sense to develop a support network and use the extra time gained from not monitoring to helping employees grow in their problem solving abilities.

A manager who acts as a catalyst will identify the tools holding consultants at bay and work to eliminate those obstacles. Amid the 1980s management fads that passed, one strong point emerged: eliminate work duplication. Work to make tools efficient so employees have more time to spend with their customers. Allow the computer to do menial tasks and design programs that automatically reduce the work amount done by the employee. In the workplace, the employee is the master and the slave is the computer, not vice versa.

Employees need to know the goals. Management needs to establish expectations and provide feedback based on stated objectives. Coaching is the process of identifying needs based on stated goals, performance, and the employee's perception of what he or she needs. If the employee understands the components of quality outcomes, he or she can develop their own personal game plan to reach those goals. Excellence and quality become the norm, not the goals.

When expectations are not met in the work environment, many managers blame the workforce and the education they received. Poor results are a convoluted collection of poorly defined objectives, ideas, and processes that may or may not be in the control of the manager. It takes great leadership and patience to turn a work environment that feels lost into one that produces positive results.

Implementation

Give your consultants the objectives and let them figure out the implementation. For less talented employees, create remedial training that is more specialized and less demanding than the top groups' responsibility. If new employees can experience success on intermediary levels, perhaps they can graduate to more challenging roles. Either way, create success and protect the company from inadequacy on the phone with a customer.

Sparky Anderson, a baseball manager recently elected to the Baseball Hall of Fame, is the only manager to have won the World Series title in both leagues. He held a press conference after the announcement he was being elected to the "Hall." During this media conference, he discussed the two types of managers in baseball. He stated managers are either "smart" or "stupid." Stupid managers were the result of believing they could take teams with little talent and lead them to championships. They struggle with these unskilled teams until they are fired. Smart managers surround themselves with talented ball players. The smart manager then sits back, keeps out of their way, and lets them perform. Sparky Anderson thought he was a smart manager because he had talented players and stayed out of their way.

Another baseball manager, Jim Leyland, would probably say he has been on both sides of the smart/stupid managerial fence. In 1986, the struggling Pittsburgh Pirates hired Leyland as manager. The team had fallen on hard times because of drug scandals, poor trades, and a farm system that failed to restock the club with quality players. Leyland must have felt like the "sacrificial lamb" as the team was woeful during his first two years.

Some talent started to arrive in Pittsburgh and in 1988 the team challenged the archrival New York Mets for the division crown. By 1990, the Pirates were one of the best teams and dominated their division for the next four seasons. Was Jim Leyland a "stupid" manager in 1986 and a "smart" manager in 1990? No, he was the same manager with a talented team.

Fast-forward to 1997, Jim Leyland is now the Florida Marlins manager. The team was loaded with talent and marched into the World Series against the Cleveland Indians. Two powerhouse teams played an exciting series that the Marlins eventually won. Leyland was celebrated as baseball's most respected manager. Then the roof caved in again.

The Florida owner satisfied with the one title dismantled the team and the talent was gone. The Marlins lost over one hundred games and became the first team to win a World Series and be so deplorable the next year. Leyland was disgusted and left the Marlins for the Colorado team. Was Leyland "smart" in 1997 and "stupid" in 1998? No, he lost the talent that propelled the team to greatness; he was the same person.

The important lesson for managers is to surround themselves with talent and educate employees to the maximum. Then stand back and let them perform and excel.

Listening

Soft skill training should focus on conversational skills, particularly listening. If the employee is in sales, listening skills sharpen the identification of customer needs. If the employee is in service, listening skills sharpen problem identification and ultimately the resolution. Albert Einstein stated that identifying the problem is the problem. Training programs are focused on teaching quantitative information because it takes less time to train. Teaching listening skills is time-consuming and requires an educator with teaching skills that reflect listening training.

Listening skills include paraphrasing and reflection. Paraphrasing is a summary of what was said by the customer helping clarify the need. By repeating the conversation in summary form, the consultant and the customer agree on what has been said. The customer clarifies any misinformation while the employee can continue to build an informational database to identify the problem.

Reflection

Reflection is a skill identifying emotion and reflecting it back to the customer. A customer having a disappointing experience with a product could express anger, disappointment, disgust, or perhaps inadequacy. The employee who identifies the emotion will go far in diffusing a customer's negative perception. Repairing customer relations begins with a caring employee listening to the customer.

Stress Management

There once was a person in history nicknamed "Typhoid Mary" who spread the deadly disease unknowingly from person to person. Sometimes a manager becomes a "Typhoid Mary" by causing stress from person to person. It is not productive to manage minutia; it bottlenecks creativity and new solutions and becomes a source of conflict. As a result, stress increases and growth is impaired. You need to state the organization goals, educate, and get out the way.

A key skill set overlooked in the new-hire training process includes stress management. Stress management skills allow employees to visualize quality outcomes. Most professional athletes, as they prepare for game situations, use visualization. Allowing themselves to mentally train for the moment, athletes are mentally conditioned to deal with stressful situations. Sports heroes are created long before the contest is held. Visualization is practiced daily because, like any skill, it can quickly fade.

Think about situations "played out in the mind's eye" that lead to positive outcomes. Asking for a raise, new job responsibilities, confrontation with a coworker or manager, and interviewing for new positions are scenarios visualization serves well.

Use visualization to prepare for customers who are upset. Picture what the customer might say and how they may respond. Allowing the "camera to roll," appropriate wording can develop that will diffuse a bad scenario and establish the customer's confidence once again.

Stress management is also about altering reality perceptions. Visualization can help people pick more positive outcomes but perception controls stress and allows increased productivity. Each person perceives situations differently; hence the same reality creates anxiety to some and no response to others. Defining the importance of the situation begins to address how to manage perceptions. To paraphrase Shakespeare, "the situation is not good or bad, but the mind makes it so."

Suppose you are driving on one of the many interstates or freeways that cross the countryside. As traffic begins to slow because of increased volume, you sense you will be trapped in your current lane behind a slow driver. At this point you are faced with two options. First, you can accept the situation and insert a music

CD you enjoy. You'll chalk this time up as necessary to relieve stress or time to prepare for the daily meetings.

The second choice is to get angry and begin screaming at the driver in front of you or just at drivers in general. You start pounding the steering wheel and get angry at the radio for too much talking and not enough music. The situation is the same (time was not an issue), yet two responses are made by thousands of commuters every day. The first is to relax; the second is to be irate. Your reality perception is the key to controlling stress.

COACH'S CHALKBOARD

Provided you won't hurt anybody or yourself, make yourself mad. Think of some situation or person that can get you to the point of frothing and spewing obscenities. Do you feel your pulse quicken, your palms get sweaty, or your face get flushed? You would if you were actually mad. It's the body's natural response known as "flight or fight." At one time, stress management was to either stand and fight or run for the hills. In today's workplace, it is not appropriate to do either response. Do you recall the scene from *A League of Their Own* where the baseball manager played by Tom Hanks tells a distraught player that there's no crying in baseball? In the workplace there is no room for fist or tears. Hence, stress builds because there is no energy release.

Physical activity is a positive way of controlling stress and disposing of the negative energy. Walking, running, cycling, and weight lifting are outlets that create a positive result. Not only does the day's stress dissolve, but also you are now in a better position to resist future stressful events. Eating can relieve stress but the extra weight can be detrimental to overall health. Smoking seems to relax some people, but again the health outcomes can be disastrous. Alcohol is definitely a relaxant, but can only be used sparingly and certainly not at work! So, exercise is the best choice to satisfy the need of fight or flight.

Stress is also a response to fear, or not having sufficient expertise or information. Simplifying support systems builds people's confidence and by sharing job information the company alleviates the unknown. As an acronym, fear stands for false evidence appearing real. Fear is a real enemy in a learning environment. The late educator W. Edwards Deming identified the removal of fear as one of his fourteen points for creating a more productive environment.

Organizational Skills

Organizational skills are necessary because the new workplace asks the consultant to quickly seek answers. One sidebar issue employees must deal with is speed. A customer may have initiated the call, but once he or she clears the queue, they want results. The complexity of the call may take twenty minutes to resolve. The manager wants it done in less than six minutes. It seems absurd that there would be an "occupancy" standard (on the phone instead of "logged off" to complete supporting work). This standard forces the phone representa-

tive to keep the customer on the phone while they resolve the problem. This wastes the customer's time,
gives the company a bad image for inefficiency, and
wastes money (toll-free cents per minute).

Many times the workplace establishes a hierarchy
creating dependency on the next supervision level. The
consultant asks the team manager who asks the supervisor who asks the general manager who asks the director
and so on. By the time the employee has an answer the
customer is gone. Create independent thinkers who
problem solve using the company's resources. Teach
people how to find these resources.

COACH'S CHALKBOARD

In the game of football (both college and the pros), a
clock measures time between plays. From the end of
one play to the hike of the next play, a quarterback has
less than thirty seconds to successfully call a play,
change his mind, reset the team, and initiate the play.
This need for quick and decisive action is the difference
between success and failure.

The ability to accomplish quick decisions is a result
of excellent coaching, practice, and game interactions
with the coaches. If your workplace has the need for
speed, create a game plan, practice its implementation,
and use computer simulations to provide "just-in-time"
learning modules. It is not likely that the employee has
only thirty seconds, but most centers want the call to
end in three minutes. Speed is a result of clearly defined

objectives and people with sufficient experience to implement a plan of action.

Problem Solving

Problem solving is another skill set that needs attention. Talented people know how to solve problems, just give them the resources and stand back. People need guidance on how to use resources productively. It is like watching two students studying for a test. The A student seems to know how to organize his or her thoughts. The resources become instruments for fine-tuning. They have also figured out what the instructor is looking for in terms of understanding. Add these components together and the student never fears an examination.

The B student works much harder, spending more time trying to capture the material. The B student has not learned how to refine their thinking to be more productive in a shorter time period. They know the instructor somewhat and cannot always estimate what the examination may cover. It is frustrating and stressful to know the B student worked harder but achieved a lower mark.

Teaching problem solving is not as efficient as teaching facts, features, and benefits. It requires more classroom time and an instructor who understands the need for experiential learning. Time in real life with experienced coaches is necessary to teach problem solving. Many companies do not expend resources on developing such labor-intensive training to accomplish moderate success. They are locked into the training model that there will be winners and losers (just like school) and that there are limited financial resources available.

Customers want personalized service and a long-term relationship with the service provider. This relationship depends on employees who are responsive, innovative, and can adapt to a number of situations. This environment type needs leadership more like a partner than a boss. The value is to create, not to control.

Top Of The Third

To be successful, it is important that people care. Caring is the cornerstone of responsibility. When people care about their loved ones, they take responsibility for their health and well-being. When people care about their job and the people in the workplace, they will take responsibility to achieve quality outcomes. Responsibility cannot be legislated or increased through incentives. Many managers use their positional leadership to force responsibility on their employees; they call it empowerment. Most people see through this 1980s buzzword and passively resist because they do not care about empowerment or their manager. Remember, people don't leave a company, they leave the manager.

For those companies that wish to empower their workforce, consider that empowerment is a personal choice. Show the employee the plan, the objectives, the incentives, and his or her role. Empowerment results when that individual chooses to implement the plan as designed. The people who reject the plan should find another project or a different company. They will be of no use to the company or to the company's customers if they reject the mission and vision.

Caring is an individual effort. Talented people seem to know this and display genuine caring for the workplace. This caring attitude will guide them to a leadership role. From a manager's perspective, caring is treating people as individuals. Group rules tend to punish or inhibit talented employees. This leads to frustration and people leave. Any change in organizations requires a paradigm shift in corporate culture, particularly a change from groups to individuals.

The word paradigm comes from the Greek word paradeigma, meaning model or pattern. Paradigms are rules and procedures that form boundaries and outline what it takes to reach a goal within the boundaries. Social paradigms allow us to interact with people without being offensive. Approximately forty years ago, Rosa Parks challenged the southern social paradigms by sitting near the front of the bus.

In medicine, a paradigm shift occurred in treating high blood pressure. Before the advent of the blood pressure control pill, physicians told their patients to get bed rest to control their pressure. Clearly, rest was not the right solution and medications were the best choice. Reality changed for thousands of physicians who needed to alter how they treated high blood pressure. It was a significant emotional event for both the doctor and his or her patient.

In business, "it doesn't work that way here" or "that is not part of the corporate culture" are paradigm realities. Creating a caring and responsible workforce will lessen the chance that these growth deterrents will have a long life. When an employee cares, he or she returns more calls, answers more emails, puts in extra effort in seeking solutions, and looks to help others become successful.

A tennis coach understands the value of individuality. Tennis is an individual sport where creative approaches to the game are displayed. The game strategy changes based on the playing surface, the opponent, the fatigue factor, and sometimes — plain silliness. A tennis coach understands sport individuality and knows they would fail if they tried to impose structure. Imagine a tennis team where everyone plays the same strategy because of one person!

Employees are like a tennis team and require individual game plans. A successful manager regularly interviews his or her team to define goals, objectives, motivators, and needs. A plan is then built around this discussion enhancing the employee's chance for success. In this scenario, what are the chances the employee will be passive about their work in the future?

Mentors

Mentors are important because they extend the circle of caring. They demonstrate how to be successful in the workplace. They offer tips on efficiency, the corporate culture, problem solving as it relates to the position, and consistently model quality outcomes. Mentors also model intangibles such as stress management, humor on the job, control when placed in argumentative positions, and networking among employees and management personnel.

A mentor gives the new employee a friend and confidant. To help retention rates, it is important during the first few days for new employees to have someone to talk with. The mentor also begins to understand and learn the new person's needs for the future motivational process.

Choose mentors that display the behaviors necessary in the workplace. The mentor should be knowledgeable, articulate, thorough, and have a track record of consistent quality outcomes. The mentor should earn financial incentives for the training process that would also include residuals for the new person's work and their length of employment. When not mentoring, the person blends back into the workforce. This keeps the mentor current with customers' needs.

Coaches

The coach is the next expertise level helping the new employee. The mentor on the other hand provides "macro-education," the coach will provide "micro-education." Micro-education fine-tunes knowledge, skills, attitude, and intangibles solidifying excellence. Coaching is a new intervention level building improvement plans based on the employee's perceived needs. Coaching continues to work on the fundamentals as they relate to quality. Even the great Michael Jordan had a personal coach throughout his illustrious career.

Coaches are not "doers" but work from the learner's perspective. Again the process is not laced with efficiency because discovery learning can be time consuming. Coaches who "do" will speed up the process in the short-term but in the long run slow the potential growth of the learner.

Quality coaches are talented individuals. They understand the goal and the necessary requirements for reaching the goal. They recognize talent in others and know how to use it effectively. They can also express themselves clearly to others on how to reach the goal.

Championship sports teams are not only well stocked with talented athletes; they also have quality coaches. The loss of a coach to another team can have a ripple effect, lowering the overall team performance. The late Weeb Ewbank, head coach of the Baltimore Colts and New York Jets won only one Super Bowl (Joe Namath was the quarterback). Some of his coaching "off spring" included Tom Landry and Don Shula, arguably two of the best coaches the sport has ever had. Imagine the expertise the Jets would have enjoyed if Landry and Shula had stayed with Ewbank? How many Super Bowls might a team have won with that trio as a coaching staff? By the way, that Super Bowl win came against one of Shula's best teams ever in Super Bowl III.

With coaching as a mainstay in so many facets of life, it is amazing how many companies fail to embrace this concept in the workplace. Of course, those same companies would argue their management staffs are the coaches. Managers are not usually trained as coaches. Management people often have a different agenda that includes efficiency and occupancy time, not coaching. Managers can be catalysts with their employees by making sure that the right tools are available and that company politics do not slow the team's quest for excellence.

Summary

Mentors attempt to take the new employee from the training room to the customer. Mentors are the incubators for applying learning and using problem solving skills. Coaches identify needs, create improvement plans, track motivational factors, and apply advanced skills to the learning process. Both coaches and mentors are responsible for the new employee's integration into the workplace.

It is ironic that everyday people lead complex lives making vital decisions affecting their futures; yet, at work they are treated like children. Managers set limits as to what decisions are appropriate; other decisions are escalated to the next person in the chain of command. The extent and quality of customer satisfaction is limited by a fear of making a mistake.

Top Of The Fourth

COACH'S CHALKBOARD

Retaining talented people is a major issue for companies in today's marketplace. Retaining the right people has a two-fold positive outcome:

1. The company realizes significant return on investment by reducing the need for new-hire orientation and training.
2. The customers are better served, thereby increasing their loyalty and word of mouth marketing.

Talented people need recognition for their contributions to the organization through better pay, praise, individual benefits (motivational items discovered by the manager and coach), and increased responsibility.

Statistically, in a large group, the group tends to form a normal, bell-shaped curve where the middle (or average) is defined. If you plot a group on a bell-shaped curve and have at least thirty subjects, a manager would see approximately 60 percent of the group is around the midpoint. If knowledge and skills are the barriers, training may be able to address the needs of this population.

The real worry is the lower 10 to 20 percent. These employees are killing your customer service center. If your center has two hundred employees, as many as forty people are draining the energy out of the workplace and ruining the company's image with your the customer. Move these people away from your customers and give them support jobs. Theoretically, you should not miss these people in the lower 10 to 20 percent.

Another statistical oddity suggests that 20 percent of your employees will do 80 percent of the work. On this end of the curve are your top people. Do everything possible to retain these employees. They have knowledge, skills, attitude, efficiency, effectiveness, and other intangible qualities (such as leadership) that other companies covet. These are the people you want your CEO to call when he or she has a service problem. These are the people you ask to be on display when someone makes a site visit. This group is so good that you will weep if they decide to leave you for somebody else!

In the movie *Wayne's World,* when the main characters saw a media idol, they fell to their knees, bowed to the floor, and stated, "We are not worthy." While such extremes are comical, the point remains, how often do managers praise their best employees with open displays of gratitude? Managers labor over the lower half hoping they can be salvaged. As a result, two groups lose. The lower half cannot close the gap and the upper half slides to the center. Now the customer service center is mediocre and the best will leave to pursue working with true leadership.

Resource expenditures for education are limited so why not offer education as a perk to the best employees? The return on investment of moving a poor performing group from low to middle is not as great as investing in excellence. What about those intangibles, such as leadership, that energize a workplace? It's not likely to be generated by the lower half of the curve. The lower half of the curve likes micro-management because anything that goes wrong is the manager's fault and they are quick to point this out in public. As a group, it cares little about the workplace and shuns responsibility.

Quantitative evaluations focus on averages. It is simple math any manager can perform with a calculator. After all, not many people enjoyed college statistics! So the manager takes the highs and lows, adds them up, and divides by the number in the group. This is an exciting fourth grade project! Unfortunately, the whole workforce is now measured against mediocrity.

Imagine instead of a normal, bell-shaped curve, you are looking for a positively skewed curve. This means your staff is several standard deviations above mediocrity and the competition is for the part of the curve (the tail) moving closer to perfection. What kind of customer impact will this scenario produce?

Research has never shown that customers leave a company because of long wait times to have their call answered. They leave companies because when someone did answer the phone—no quality existed. Your call center may have fewer people, but those that remain are excellent. The money saved by reducing the workforce to quality employees is used to pay those people not to leave. Education, mentoring, and coaching are now used to increase each person's stake in quality outcomes.

The people you terminated will be hired elsewhere, probably by the competitor's service center. As a result, you have an excellent staff and your competition is bogged down with trying to educate people to mediocrity. As a manager, your chances for success rise considerably. As a company, your customers will love you.

Retention of the right people is not always about money. One of the premier home-run hitters in major league baseball recently signed a contract for 36 million dollars less just so he could be closer to home. Recognition and praise are excellent alternatives to money. People enjoy a challenge and they like to be recognized for their achievement attempts. Failure should be celebrated as much as success to reinforce the idea that attempts to reach excellence are not always going to succeed. Thomas Edison failed hundreds of times before creating the light bulb. When his house burned down, a reporter asked if he was upset about losing all his research. Edison responded it was a chance for a fresh start. Failures are learning experiences that help point people in the right direction. Managers need to cele-brate every effort as much as positive results.

Behavioral research indicates that to change a sub-ject's behavior requires four statements of praise for each critical statement. Business studies indicate the ratio of praise to criticism is 1:2! Imagine the results if mentors, coaches, and managers worked on an 8:1 ratio. Caring is sharing appreciation with people. If responsi-bility is linked to caring, what is the point of holding back praise?

Top Of The Fifth

Several years ago, Robert was hired to manage a major customer service center—one of several owned by a national company. The center's purpose was to provide a variety of service requests; sales opportunities were limited. Robert was in charge of approximately two hundred service representatives. As the year progressed, the company continued its substantial growth. This customer service center was the crown jewel for the company's quest for success.

Upper management's opinion was that service calls, which dominated in call volume, should be a potential for more sales. After all, once a customer has had their problem solved, it should be easy to segue to other communication products. Upper management called Robert and suggested that more sales were possible. The company gave Robert the directive to produce an increase in sales.

Robert, believing upper management was right, went about determining what it was going to take to reach the goal. After crunching the numbers, Robert determined the percent increase that upper management desired would take an additional six sales per person per day. Well, that didn't seem unreasonable at all. Six sales from the eighty or so calls received daily by each person would be easy. Some people would even exceed that number producing even more sales and recognition for Robert.

Robert envisioned great possibilities from this opportunity. He was being given a chance to show he had potential for a vice-president position, if not with the current company, certainly with someone else. They would be banging the doors down trying to recruit him. He was sure the other customer service center managers were envious of his assignment.

Robert called a staff meeting and announced his program to the supervisors and team managers. Upper management needed more sales and this center was selected to lead the charge. Everyone should be honored and Robert was sure everyone in the room appreciated the assignment implications. The sales numbers were not unreasonable: only six more sales per day per person.

Robert felt, and so did the management staff, that the numbers were achievable. The reasonable goal, coupled with the attractive discounts, should get everybody excited. In the sales matured areas, heavy marketing would be used to generate even more interest, so the sales should blossom. The managers were excited and prepared to deliver the necessary numbers. The management team went to the workforce to deliver the message after the meeting. Robert retired to his office to crunch more numbers and prepare a trend line.

After three months, sales had reached 50 percent of the goal. Robert was upset. How could these representatives not meet such an easy goal as six sales per day? Robert called a meeting with the management team for their input. The supervisors responded that a number of issues on the floor were causing problems. First, the representatives didn't feel it was their job to sell.

Second, the representatives didn't feel they had sufficient training to sell the products. They were not comfortable talking to the customers about additional items. Third, the representatives saw their job as providing service to customers.

The supervisors had done their job by "getting on them" to sell more aggressively. They felt the training department had let the organization down because the representatives were no better today in sales as compared to three months ago. Everyone agreed that most of the representatives would have met their goals if they had been provided with better training and incentives.

Robert was less angry at this point and began to chart a new course of action. He still felt the goal was fair, particularly with marketing's aggressive campaigns and lower prices. He would contact upper management for incentive money to support increased sales.

He would talk to training about a more aggressive training program.

He asked the managers to deliver "pep" talks about the importance of the sales quota and the center's role in the growing realm of the company. All that was needed was a little more incentive, a clearly defined goal to "shoot for" and trainers who understood the importance of the program. The meeting ended upbeat.

The third quarter ended and the numbers tallied. Robert was in disbelief. Despite an increase in incentive dollars per sale, regularly scheduled training programs, and constant prodding by the supervisors, sales never reached the goal. The best month only hit 85 percent of the goal! Robert was obsessed with finding an answer. Upper management was getting impatient and some of the other centers were beating his group, despite a lower call volume. The other centers overshadowed Robert's "crown jewel" vision.

A meeting was called and Robert announced his ultimatum. He was no longer going to be "Mr. Nice Guy." Things were going to be different starting today. He had a poor performers list. They would all be placed in the center's Team Improvement Program and they would have two months to meet the goals or face termination.

The training department was going to be revamped by terminating several people and replacing them with vendors that know how to produce sales people. By year's end, the center would be meeting its goal or there would be new faces everywhere!

The plan now had two essential points. First, upper management would be contacted and told about the incompetence of the training department. Robert would recommend the group be eliminated except for one person. He would also like to contract with an outside source for sales training.

Second, he wanted to "thin the herd" and rid the center of its poor performers and improve the center with fresh people. Robert sent upper management a plan and proceeded without a formal response from management.

The supervisors would "crack" down. If a person made the daily goal, they would push for more. They were told to act even tougher on those people going to the Team Improvement Program. The goal was for them to shape up or get out. The supervisors were also expendable and if their teams failed to reach the goal, they would be demoted or terminated.

The word got out and the representatives were told they would meet the goal (which had been increased to eight sales per day in order to make up for the poor performers) or lose their job. The reaction from the representatives was much different than expected.

First, a few people immediately put in their resignations. These were not the poor performers; the group represented some of the best service representatives in the center. A competitor immediately hired them. Second, the remaining representatives notified a local union they wanted intervention.

The thought that the union could dictate how the company runs its customer service centers made upper management queasy. The organization's crown jewel was now in turmoil with people quitting, getting terminated, and a union threat. This was not acceptable to upper management.

The first step was for the CEO and upper management to visit the center. The possibility that the representatives would vote in a union was real and had a good chance of succeeding. The CEO was the first to go and speak with the representatives.

During the first few days, the CEO called meetings and discussed the representatives' concerns. They never saw their role as sales people and they felt betrayed. They were excellent service representatives with a good track record of taking care of customers. The representatives never had input. They knew if they passively resisted the goals would not be met and the plan would fail. They thought the company would get rid of Robert; they never expected to see their friends leave or be terminated. Their resistance had backfired and they wanted to get even by calling in the union.

The CEO knew he had little time to act, as the union vote was only several weeks away. He had to act decisively to win back his representatives. In a scene reminiscent of the French Revolution, heads would roll.

Whack! Management fired Robert.

Whack! Two supervisors with "notorious" reputations were fired.

Whack! No more sales quotas were required for this group.

Whack! An immediate one-dollar per hour raise for everyone.

Whack! The Team Improvement Program was eliminated and new trainers would be hired from the existing group of representatives.

The CEO handpicked a manager who would report directly to him. There were no repercussions for the representatives who wanted the union and those who were terminated were offered their job again.

The union vote lost by less than ten votes. The company prevailed and "dodged the proverbial bullet." Sacrifices and a large amount of money were spent to correct the course of the organization to make everything right again. A new manager, Carolyn, was selected from a lengthy search that took almost eight months. Carolyn, whose personality was the opposite of Roberts, reported directly to the CEO. No sales quotas were required and people "from the ranks" were promoted into management and training jobs.

The call center has since gone over many months with no further incidences or talk of a union. It is no longer the "crown jewel" of the company. Other centers have surpassed its value to the company. Carolyn is Milquetoast and people have no opinion as to her value. The company may look at the center in the future and question its continued operation.

Robert relocated and took another job as a service center manager. He still feels betrayed by his old company; he was just following orders. When he needed upper management to support him, they terminated him. As a result, he had to take a pay cut, uproot his family to a new location, and lost money on the sale of his original house. It was a bitter experience.

COACH'S CHALKBOARD

A leader does not choose followers. Followers choose leaders based on the mutual respect and acceptance of the leader's mission and vision. This was the crux of the problem with Robert and his ultimate failure. The "trickle down" chain of command met with resistance from the workforce because they didn't accept the mission or want Robert's vision. Robert assumed people were on his team because they worked in the environment. Taking the need to reach new sales goals to the frontline representatives would have potentially yielded a productive outcome. This is the organizational mistake made by "Roberts" everywhere. It is necessary to treat your employees as though they were your customers.

Robert failed to meet with people at every level. The group never betrayed him; they just didn't see sales as their mission. Since Robert never received the group's approval, hard-line tactics only created more distance. Robert sacrificed his job because he failed to be a leader.

Did Robert deserve his fate? His vision of success was at the expense of others. His motivation was driven by personal recognition and the potential that others in the organization would be envious of his success. This is not leadership and the workforce will reject this kind of leader.

In any given sport season, you will read about managers or coaches who are fired. The primary reason given is that the person lost his or her effectiveness in communicating with the team (players learning of coaching decisions through the media, for example). Hence, the team fails to respond and underachieves against opponents. As a fan, won't you agree that managers deserve their fate when the team is losing? Robert's upper management had to terminate him in order to restore the confidence of the workforce.

Recently, the Pittsburgh Pirates fired their general manager following nine straight losing seasons and the team is now well on their way to a tenth losing season. In his press conference, the general manager stated that the club would not likely find anyone who worked as hard and put in as much time as he did over the past nine years. Just like Robert, this person missed the point: It is not about time or instilling a sense of urgency. It is about achieving quality outcomes using a plan and leadership.

What will you do if faced with similar circumstances?

List several ideas about how you would get acceptance for a new idea or campaign?

What would be your plan? List some of your key
thoughts:

Top Of The Sixth

A medical surgical laser uses light to cut or vaporize human tissue. Unlike Dr. Evil who planned to use a laser to destroy Washington, D.C., in a recent movie comedy, medical lasers are precise instruments using minimal light focal lengths for effectiveness. Lasers are such a fine-tuned point of light that "lasers are to light as music is to noise."

Laser light begins in a tube activated by an electrical pulse. The pulse reacts with a gas or inert material (crystals) to create a population of photons. At each end of the tube, a mirror reflects the bouncing photons back and forth until a beam of light is formed. The beam intensity is a result of the synergy of wave-like patterns building on each other, creating a powerful medical or industrial tool.

The beam of light is then passed through a series of mirrors that maintain the intensity and small diameter (measured in microns). In medicine, the beam is focused on the tissue and activated and then the light proceeds to cut, vaporize, coagulate, or be absorbed (killing unwanted tissue cells over time). If the beam is aimed at a surface several feet away, it loses its power because the beam begins to divert again.

You can compare laser light to people in work environments. Light begins as scattered, multi-directional harmless beams. The mirrors in the laser tube stimulate and amplify the light waves to create a powerful instrument. Light is created when an electron releases a photon as it returns to its original orbit around the nucleus. Everything dynamic will seek to return to its resting state.

In work environments, it is easy to have people not focused. Employees worry about software, continuing education, their families, irate callers, and so on. Managers need to keep the workforce focused on the customer's needs (just like the laser's mirrors). Also, if the workforce is stimulated and produces energy, eventually that momentum will relax and seek to return to a less dynamic environment. Energy has been released; therefore, the key is what did management do to make progress during this time frame? Understand that this relaxation is natural and necessary before the next surge can occur.

While technology struggles to be more consumer friendly, customer service centers have become the education center in addition to service issues. To build customer loyalty, companies are turning to their service employees. If the telephones were as complicated to use as computers, people would still be using Morse code.

Customers are not spending time in a service queue for a simple answer. Customer's questions revolve around the information they need the most:

1. More education to maximize product use,
2. Innovative ways to broaden product use and,
3. Why the product is not working to their expectations.

It is employee availability, a live voice in a high-tech world that makes the difference to a customer. People answering phones are the company's most important resource and will generate greater profits. Retention of talented employees is so important that in some companies managers are sent to training programs to learn how to increase retention.

Consultant is an appropriate term as these phone agents are educating, advising, and troubleshooting. Customer loyalty is built by how well they learn multiple uses for the product and the ultimate value it offers. Many companies, including car manufacturers, are including videotapes to help the customer learn efficient and safe product use. Videotapes cannot beat the live voice of a consultant, even if it is over a phone line. Top-shelf companies put their best people in these front-line situations.

Top-shelf companies realize customer service center positions are a career opportunity and not simply entry-level. To educate a customer over the phone takes a special set of skills like visualization, clear diction, appropriate speed of instruction, and listening for understanding. Less talented service consultants read from an instruction sheet without a clue as to how their message is received. Less talented consultants fail to see the importance of having the consumer product in their home so they can sense what the customer is saying.

Layering the customer service center can help develop the quality outcomes a manager is seeking. Initially, mentors are the best people to work with new employees. As the first group graduates, some mentors take over as coaches. Some of the best new employees are elevated to training as a mentor and the process continues until the center is fully supported. Having employees involved in the education process is the surest way to help them understand what needs to be learned.

Another approach is to create teams that will address service components. A team may include a coach and/or mentor, a person skilled in educating over the phone, a software expert, an order-entry person, and an informational resource person. The team takes calls and the call is directed to the person best suited to a quality outcome with respect to the caller's problem.

Forward thinking will move companies from constructing facilities for customer service centers to contracting with people to work from their homes. In addition to the savings from not having to maintain a building, companies will save money by having less management and benefit issues such as sick time, vacation time, day care centers, or parking problems. They will also use locally based representatives that will save on the toll-free number expenses. The Internet and virtual private networks will enable millions of people to work from their home office. This decentralization move is the critical point behind hiring leadership instead of management.

THE FUTURE ACCORDING
to the BUREAU of LABOR STATISTICS

If the Bureau of Labor Statistics is accurate for the period through 2008, customer service centers will be inundated with people seeking training for appropriate skills in the new workplace. Some of the key points made by a variety of research documents include:

1. A 14 percent growth in employment through 2008
2. Over 50 percent of the growth will be the result of current workers retiring or transferring to other occupations
3. The need for workers in service related organizations is expected to increase much faster than the average growth across all industries
4. Short-term, on-the-job training will be the norm for 60 percent of the occupations with the largest numerical growth
5. Women in the workplace will reach 48 percent saturation by 2008; additionally, nearly half of this group will be forty-five years or older.

6. Nearly half of the available workforce will only have a high school diploma and more than one-third will lack the reading, writing, and math skills needed for the workplace. Further, with respect to educational attainment, high school graduates are twice as likely to be unemployed as compared to the same age group with a bachelor's degree.

7. Finally, the workplace is becoming more complex. From 1996 to 1998, the American Management Association reported that the failure rate of reading and math skills increased from 19 percent to 36 percent. The report attributed the failures to more complex job skills instead of schools' failure to teach the necessary skills.

For further reading, use the following links:
http://stats.bls.gov/ocohome.html (Occupational
        Outlook Handbook)
http://stats.bls.gov/pub/ooq/ooqhome.htm
        (Occupational Outlook Quarterly)

http://stats.bls.gov (employment, occupation and
        related information)
www.ajb.dni.us (America's Job Bank)
www.acinet.org (America's career infonet)
www.alx.org (America's Learning Exchange)
www.bls.gov/opub/mlr/mlrhome.htm (Monthly Labor
        Review)
www.amanet.org/research (American Management

Association survey info regarding basic reading skills)

www.nelc.org (National Employer Leadership Council)

http://stats.bls.gov/cghome.htm (Career Guide to Industries)

http://stats.bls.gov/oes/msa/oessrch1.htm (Occupational Employment Statistics, earnings data)

http://stats.bls.gov/compub.htm (National Compensation Survey)

Top Of The Seventh

Many companies claim they have a learning organization because they do orientation, training, and offer on-going seminars or classes. A learning organization is more than classes and instructors. It is an environment where learning occurs spontaneously from every employee level. A learning environment flows with ideas that solve organizational needs from a variety of directions. Several teams may be working on the same problem from different angles. At the same time, other teams are wrestling with other needs. If a roadblock is encountered, the teams move in different directions, perhaps tackling new problems, but there is always energy from learning. The teams do not shut down because of political roadblocks. Leadership addresses the issue of company politics. The teams gain strength from the fact they are trusted. The workplace is dynamic, filled with creative energy, and has little resemblance to the traditional linear (step-by-step) approach to learning found in many companies. Teams find ways to "leap-frog" to solutions and are proactive, like a surfer riding the crest of a wave.

In a learning environment, the boundaries are constantly shifting but the goal is always in sight. The manager as a catalyst keeps the workplace focused and provides insight to the company direction. He or she is the communication arm of the learning group and keeps upper management excited about potential outcomes.

The company's mission helps provide focus in a dynamic workplace that always has a touch of chaos. The mission is the goal line and is definable regardless of the surrounding milieu. The workplace vision provides motivation to the group as they work to create quality outcomes. A workplace without a mission and vision is like music is to noise.

A learning environment maximizes communication, interaction, participation, shared information, and resources at all levels. The idea of the "silo hierarchy" with its turf mentality is lost in a learning organization. Creative employees busy popping corks don't have much time to play corporate games. A learning environment creates excellence and winning attitudes because it is not designed to create winners and losers. Talented people have no time for losing and are not interested in competitions where losers are created. They don't want to see their coworkers and friends labeled as "losers."

A learning environment is fun. A learning environment will attract additional talented people. Opportunities will draw talented people to the company. Leadership is practiced and those who want to be leaders come to be mentored. This explains why sports camps are so popular. If the camp has recognizable coaching names, the waiting list creates a name backlog that may take years to fulfill.

A learning environment embraces failed attempts as part of the learning process. Excellence is the retention of working ideas. This commitment to an experimental approach leads to innovation and greater success. It also speeds up the process to make the workplace more responsive to the customer's needs.

Minimize the Peter Principle

Some people learn at an early age that cigarette smoking can be pleasurable. As they grow older, the pleasure becomes an addiction and quitting is impossible. People believe the "bad" things that happen to people who smoke will happen to someone else. Smokers believe the research is slanted to get them to stop and everybody dies of something anyway. Rationalization of facts and justification of continuing with a habit or thought pattern is known as "cognitive dissonance."

People use cognitive dissonance for a variety of reasons to justify their actions. Lottery players believe they can beat the odds and win substantial amounts of money. People will buy additional accessories for an expensive automobile because of cognitive dissonance. Managers believe they should be promoted and they can do the job because of cognitive dissonance. People will justify any action they believe is right. This is human nature and this is why the Peter Principle exists.

The idea that the only way to be successful is to climb the corporate ladder has led to the Peter Principle. Traditional company models are structured like pyramids, with the highest salaries near the top. The battleground is in the middle where managers and talented employees vie for the allotment of dollars in that organizational sector. If the company's mindset is that managers will always make more than the frontline consultant, the potential of retaining key consultants will be minimal. This causes people to seek promotions even when they lack the talent to be successful at a new level.

Promotions usually occur because somebody was strong at something. If it is sales, they become middle management in sales. If it is service, they become middle management in service. It is ironic that when a person is initially hired, orientation and training follow, yet when a person is promoted, training does not seem to be part of the package. This system implies that managing is intuitive, a skill that might be acquired after only several weeks of experience. As a result of poor transitional strategy, talented people become frustrated in their new role because it is poorly defined and supported.

Promotions can cost the company and the work environment in several ways. First, the aforementioned Peter Principle will lead to a person losing or leaving their job. Second, the promotion removes talented individuals from contact with the customer. This is so critical to the companies' future and appropriate replacement people are difficult to find.

Third, the leadership and resources the person provided to coworkers may be minimized because of their new job role. Fourth, conflicts can arise between the promoted individual and the manager if the manager is a positional leader. Open hostility will create "sides" and demoralize the workforce. Fifth, promoting quality people leaves openings and less-qualified people taking calls. This will require more hiring, more training classes, and less chance for return on investment (financial loss for the company).

And sixth, if scheduling is arranged by seniority, promoting the best people will leave openings for poor performers to begin interacting with customers at the most critical timeframes of the day. Once again, promotion because of past performance and the individual's need for more compensation creates an ill fit and the company and the person both lose.

The alternative is to compensate people for their value, not their position. Next, develop career paths within the workplace that will allow talented people to continue to be challenged. Mentor, coaching, and creative positions such as group consultant keep the person in contact with customers by interacting with several consultants. The idea that people burn out is a myth; rather, boredom and lack of recognition that drive discontent employees away. Creative environments can keep people energized.

Govern the Individual Instead of the Group

Positional leaders fixate on rules and apply them to the whole group. This person will experience less and less success with the current job market. Successful coaches and managers in sports treat star athletes different than the rest of the team. It is hard to replace a star performer. Consequently, that person is given more latitude. If an athlete fails to keep him or herself ready for competition, he or she is no longer a star and they lose their status. A faded star becomes expendable.

A recent movie about Howard Stern (*Private Parts*) illustrates the point of star power. Regardless if the movie is fact or fiction, the movie's media executives scorn and censor the main character because he had no audience for his show (i.e. no profit). Once Stern developed a persona that attracted an audience, he had creative control. Stern would do outrageous stunts that were in "poor taste." This made corporate executives nervous, but he made lots of money for his company and he was a star. Management treated him differently from other radio personalities. As the audience tires of his program, he will lose star status and will be forced to follow the rules like everyone else or leave.

Companies are in business to make a profit (yes, even non-profits want to make a profit). Highly talented people, "star athletes," will make you money. A middle management, positional leader is expendable. He or she does not make the company money. That person is going to micromanage your star performers right out the door. To add more insult, before the star performer leaves, they will passively resist the manager and create discord among the employees. Star performers need quality leadership to maintain their output.

To define quality leadership, include caring about the person. A quality leader is concerned foremost about the other person. The success of a leader is a result of the success of the people being led. The successful leader provides vision, a navigational plan, and allows the star performers a chance to excel. Sitting with each person and mapping a series of objectives, both people know when success is achieved or when the course needs to be altered.

Successful leaders are great communicators. They deliver bad news and take the brunt of complaints. They meet with people to discuss an action plan and seek their input. Communicators do not rely on third party people. Communicators make sure they share knowledge.

Quality leaders are unassuming and humble. Yet each quality leader leaves behind a legacy that is impossible for someone else to maintain. Who were the people that replaced Winston Churchill, Bear Bryant, Mother Theresa, or Colin Powell? How hard will it be to replace Jack Welch, Reverend Billy Graham, or Nelson Mandela? These individuals exemplify leadership and their legacies are enormous.

THE FABLE OF OL' RED

Ol' Red was a fabulous egg-laying producer. The hen easily outdistanced the other hens in productivity.

Ol' Red loved her job and took great pride in her appearance and attitude. She was a model hen.

The other hens always started very productive, but would soon lose their enthusiasm as they aged. The reason: the Old Man terminated the hens after several productive years no matter how productive they were. Needless to say, the hens counted their days and eventually they were gone.

Ol' Red was getting close to that date. The hens would whisper reminders and encourage her to take it easy and enjoy the time she had left. But Ol' Red pressed on with an attitude that never waned, setting new records.

The barnyard was not quite sure about the exact date or details, but during the week Ol' Red was to be terminated, the Old Man told Ol' Red that she would be spared if she coached the other hens to be more productive. The Old Man appreciated her effort and he thought that this opportunity would be a good way to say "thanks."

Ol' Red was flattered. She had accepted her fate but was determined to do her best and leave a legacy of accomplishment. Ol' Red went to work coaching the other hens on how to increase production. Diet, exercise, rest, and an attitude adjustment were the first fundamentals she addressed.

As productivity increased, more hens were spared. The fear that gripped the barnyard slowly disappeared. The next few months were euphoric with a level of productivity that was unparalleled in the industry.

One day, the Old Man came to the barnyard, picked up Ol' Red and left. The barnyard's enthusiasm went down like the Titanic. All that productivity and it didn't seem to matter; all hens are eventually terminated. The fear that had been contained and disappeared was now back stronger than ever.

As the hens sulked around the barnyard, a news update was broadcast. Ol' Red was now in charge of a new barnyard across the other side of the farm. It was bigger and had three times more hens. Because of the outstanding productivity, the Old Man had enough resources for expansion and he rewarded Ol' Red with a fabulous promotion.

Lil' Blue was promoted to handle the coaching chores of the old barnyard. Her job was easy, as several dozen hens could have been named coach. The hens went back to the business of building an empire, steadily increasing productivity.

Production over the two barnyards was so great that the Old Man gained enormous wealth. All of his hens lived long and fulfilling lives. Termination was a thing of the past and a scary story told to the chicks. Many of the hens retired with full benefits afforded by the barnyard.

Ol' Red eventually retired and later died peacefully in her sleep. She gave the barnyard a legacy of productivity, positive attitude, and a legion of leaders that carried on for generations.

Legacy

Companies seek leadership at the top that can lead to a legacy. Leadership can be everywhere if the climate encourages growth. If employees embrace the vision, they will seek excellence and quality outcomes. In a customer service center, each consultant is like an entrepreneur. He or she will adopt a leadership position if they know what the plan seeks to achieve. They will treat each customer as though it was their company.

It is impossible to find one person to be a primary leader. This "John Wayne" persona is too hard to develop with the enormous complexity of today's workplace and job market. Having a leadership throng provides unlimited expertise and potential solutions.

COACH'S CHALKBOARD
Developing Your Players

If you are an owner of a major league team and have designs to win championships, you build through your minor league system. You hire coaches who teach fundamentals and will be patient with future superstars as they make mistakes. The coaches cultivate a learning environment that features open communication and constant knowledge and skills improvement.

Coaches realize that every player in the minor leagues cannot make it to the big leagues, but they continue to teach and inspire. Even if the player must give up on their dream to become a big league ball player, they still need to develop a work ethic that can support them in the future. Coaches build from within, each year promoting those players displaying the talent and leadership necessary to take the next step.

Companies spend a great deal of money and time recruiting upper level management people for their company, searching for someone who can bring the necessary experiences and leadership to take the organization to the next level.

What about middle management positions? If a company takes the time necessary to cultivate a learning environment and identifies potential leaders, would you agree that the return to the company is greater than taking a chance on an unknown recruit? Consider this: would you rather place your company's future with someone who has been with the company for a period of years and has roots in the community, or someone passing through?

Just as baseball prepares for the future through its player development, so too can your company. Give people a chance to learn new knowledge and skills to complement the talent he or she brings to the workplace. Provide coaches to help people learn from his or her mistakes and build a repertoire of experiences valuable to your company.

As a sidebar, naysayers will point to the New York Yankees as the current champions of baseball and suggest its ownership "bought" the World Series titles. Naysayers will scoff at the idea of building through the minor leagues. They will say that money buys championships and companies should go out and buy what they need. But, consider the reversal of fortunes experienced by the Oakland Athletics, Chicago White enced by the Oakland Athletics, Chicago White Sox, Cincinnati Reds, Florida Marlins, San Francisco Giants and, yes, the competitive teams from Pittsburgh, Detroit, and Anaheim.

Also consider the following two stories:

In 1972, Commissioner Bowie Kuhn and several owners declared baseball to be dead, killed by free agency. Owners and fans still echo those sentiments nearly thirty years later in the wake of mega-contracts. Yet, baseball thrives as evidenced by the construction of new stadiums and attendance throughout the season. Why? The minor leagues continually supply new superstars to capture the fans' imagination and adoration. All the current superstars are the products of minor league instruction and nurturing.

Second, through the Ruth, DiMaggio, and Mantle eras, the New York Yankees appeared invincible, having the best talent of each decade. Then came a dry spell of fifteen years where the Yankees were defeated in their division. Championships in 1977 and 1978 seemed to herald the return to glory, yet the current run did not start again for over a decade. Eventually, the cycle will begin again and Yankee fans will have to wait for the next round of superstars to surface. Companies cannot afford such drastic swings between highs and lows. They need to maintain a consistency through time in order to stay competitive. Developing employees through the "minor leagues" creates the depth necessary for long-term relationships with customers.

COACH'S CHALKBOARD
Web Sites that Promote Leadership

www.eep.com (Executive Excellence Publishing)
www.leader-values.com
www.lead-edge.com
www.changedynamic.com/index.html
www.leadingconcepts.com/homepage.htm
www.srg.co.uk/
www.roberts-institute.com/home.html
www.dynamicleadership.com
www.leadership-dynamics.com
www.ccl.org (Center for Creative Leadership)
www.lmisf.com (LMI San Francisco)
www.enleadership.com
http://leadershipmanagement.com
www.leadershipiq.com/testlead.html
www.leadership_development.com/
www.leadershipcatalyst.org
www.trans-act.com/forms/leadership.htm
http://advanced-leadership.com/training.html
www.leadership.org.uk/index.html
www.leadership-online.com
www.theartofleadership.com

Top Of The Eighth

COACH'S CHALKBOARD

When a person trains a puppy, it is important never to make the dog feel as though it lost when playing a game. To earn the puppy's respect, the trainer ends the game and rewards the dog for its behavior. The owner offers praise and physical contact (a hug or handshake) to reinforce the idea that the important part of the game is not winners or losers, but the activity.

This concept of creating a win-win scenario is the failure of the pro-sports metaphor. Pro sports are about winning and creating losers. Fortunately, pro sports do not practice a consumptive attitude about winning; at least the losers do earn a salary.

Amateur athletics is about sportsmanship and playing for the admiration and respect of sports. It is about the men and women participating in 10K running events, triathlons, and softball or volleyball leagues.

Over time, no one remembers the specifics of winning or losing; they just remember that it was fun.

Work is like amateur athletics. Employees attempt to be winners and contribute to the company's success. Managers who practice strong leadership, caring, and respect help make the employees feel like winners. Employees like the feeling of responsibility, making contributions, and having fun. Over time, no one can remember exactly what happened during a given day of the workweek. But, they will only remember the day the boss made them feel like a loser.

An American Company

An American Company hired Jim as its latest person with star potential. Jim came to the company with outstanding credentials and the company immediately named him general manager for its growing customer service center.

Jim used his strengths in computer science and telephony to gain the confidence and respect of those around him. Jim was a good fit in the company's plans because of his technical background. It was an additional plus that people liked him and he seemed to fit comfortably in a variety of social settings.

The building process began and Jim started adding staff. He needed three components for his budding department so he hired from within as well as from the outside. With the core people in place, it was time to start servicing.

As with many managers seen as rising stars, Jim asked to be involved with different committees. Over the next months, he moved from a silent observer to an effective contributor.

Jim networked successfully and carefully cultivated his service staff. However, because the company thought it needed more customer service expertise, it hired Rachel as its vice-president for customer service center operations. Management asked Jim to report directly to her and use his technical expertise and experience to guide her through the operational processes. Unfortunately, Rachel's hiring moved Jim down one notch on the chain of command and eliminated his presence on several committees.

Rachel had no experience in communications, but had a strong background in customer service center management and operations. From the first meeting, Rachel and Jim collided. Jim's drive to the top had been derailed, but more importantly, he could not control "his" customer service center. Plus, Rachel had no experience in his field of expertise. Jim got some strong needling from his buddies about having to report to a woman and she knew very little about telecommunications. Rachel also resented Jim because of his reactions to her over the first several days, plus the fact he was withholding information.

Jim would talk at length to his peers about Rachel's lack of experience and "flighty" ways. Rachel was a person who attacked problems differently and saw "gray" areas while Jim saw things as "black or white."

The level of cynicism and distrust continued to grow between them.

Rachel had more to do than just deal with Jim. She needed to travel to the other customer service centers and discuss their plans. She enjoyed these trips because the other managers were more receptive. She appointed a person to stay at the corporate level to be her communication link while she was on the road. Jim would seize these opportunities to schedule meetings with upper management in which he emphasized Rachel's behavior and lack of knowledge.

Rachel did have an abrasive side because of her impatience to prove her worth to the company. Being an "outsider" kept her in a defensive posture. It also angered her when she heard about Jim's meetings with upper management while she was out of town. She was sinking fast.

Rachel decided to take her ideas directly to the representatives. This would allow her to influence more people and achieve results with her service philosophy. Rachel started meeting with the staff. Jim often called subsequent meetings in which he contradicted what Rachel had proposed. The workforce was now splitting into two camps. The first supported Rachel because she had new ideas and carried a higher rank. The other group supported Jim because they knew he had greater political clout and could eventually win.

Jim was quick to recognize his camp of followers. He designed new job titles and pay increases for his loyal followers. Rachel never countered because she never measured the impact of the continuous undermining. Rachel had a creative mind, but lacked political savvy.

Rachel was terminated at year's end. She was given a substantial separation package to get her by until she found another job. Jim was given carte blanche to run the organization the way he wanted. Jim was also given a significant raise, direct access to upper management, and an invitation to attend as many committees as he wanted.

Jim was never going to be a "victim" to an outsider again. He surrounded himself with loyal followers that never challenged his decisions. He had "fall guys" to take the blame when situations did not match upper management's expectations. He worked to create complicated routines he knew would intimidate anyone "looking over his shoulder." Whenever questioned about his decisions or programs, Jim developed an elaborate techno-speak language that caused others to not ask additional questions. Jim's star was rising again, at least from his perspective.

The quantitative results spoke volumes. Turnover hit a staggering percentage. Call volume increased, but so did wait time and call abandonment. Sales, now part of the service center, per day per person were lower in spite of a financial incentive system. The representatives seemed not to care anymore.

Many representatives passively resisted Jim's plan. It had little to do with Rachel or the company. They resented the fact that Jim had become too fixated on the concept of winners and losers. At first it seemed like a harmless series of games designed to spark enthusiasm. As time went on, it became clearer that part of the fall-out from the struggle between Rachel and Jim was a loss of camaraderie. "All for one and none for all," was the twist on the familiar rallying cry.

Jim's plan was reminiscent of the dialog spoken by actor Alec Baldwin in *Glengarry Glen Ross*: "First place sales gets a Cadillac, second place gets steak knives and third place, well there is no third place." The representatives got tired of seeing their friends humili-ated because they were in "third place." They were feel-ing defeated with no support.

Jim remains as the general manager. Jim is a politi-cal machine and is firmly entrenched. The quest for a new vice-president for the customer service centers has yielded no new person willing to walk into such a situa-tion.

Jim lost the respect of the people he needed to help him be successful. The best people left and those re-maining were afraid to express their opinion. The incentive program fails to reward much of the workforce in any given month.

Jim is as much a victim as the people he manages. He didn't start his career with this mentality. He learned this behavior through his political maneuverings. Jim's winner and loser mentality began with Rachel's hiring. When Jim found politics could advance his position, he used the winners and losers mentality to strengthen his position. Having a loyal following is part of the political process.

The Top Ten List of the Companies that Support Winners and...Winners

#10 It is a company that seeks excellence without a chain of command mentality.

#9 It has downplayed personal domains and does not have turf issues.

#8 It consists of two-way communications and ideas that flow in every direction.

#7 It has decision-making that attempts to involve everyone.

#6 It supports a team concept and never pits people against each other.

#5 It has a greater concern for employees' welfare while still meeting customer's needs.

#4 It is always truthful when selling or servicing products.

#3 Its employees are offered pay and incentives based on his or her contributions to defined outcomes.

#2 Its process of customer care is based on the representative's decision based on the collected facts instead of rules and procedures.

And number ONE:

Everyone understands the mission and vision, and everyone contributes to quality outcomes.

Pyramids

In traditional companies, the closer a person is to the top point of the pyramid, the higher the income. This position also corresponds with more responsibility and political influence. The higher position in the pyramid is also related to office space, privacy, and additional company perks. The inverse relationship is the higher the location in the pyramid, the lower the time spent with customers. Perhaps this is the origin of the phrase "Ivory Tower," denoting a mythical private space within the pyramid has little contact with the outside world.

The pyramid shape should have something to do with employee value. The lower a person is situated, the less expendable he or she becomes. In construction parlance, the wide base is necessary for support; hence, companies would see this as their least disposable area. In customer service centers, the base is the point of contact for the company's customers.

This is where the stars should reside. When talented people are allowed to leave, the company has the problem of sustaining growth on a crumbling foundation.

Think of a car racing across a desert. Unlimited speed, open territory, a full tank of gas, and the stereo cranked to high; can you feel the rush? As the car goes on its journey, there are no fueling stations, only speed and momentum. But, the car is running out of gas and despite the fast start and the high speed, it will not make its destination across the desert. There weren't any gas stations to keep the car going.

People are the fuel for companies. Only people can maintain substantial growth. If too few talented people are recruited and retained, the company will run out of fuel. Many positional leaders never realize this until it is too late.

The company had great speed in heading toward its destination. It ran out of fuel because of the pyramid. The fuel is brainpower and it is the company's greatest asset. Yet the greatest asset is buried on the bottom with little chance of affecting change because of the hierarchical structure of the pyramid.

The pyramid needs to be reconfigured to look and act more like a globe. A globe is round and can be easily navigated because a person can travel in a variety of directions and still get to their destination. A globe can also spin and travel in an orbit at the same time, allowing it to deal with change and chaos. A globe has a place for everyone. Another interesting feature about a globe is people in multiple locations are thinking about similar problems with potential solutions. Even though the people may not speak the same languages, have the same backgrounds, or report to a manager, they work passionately to achieve results. When completed, everyone embraces the answers all over the globe. And the globe just keeps spinning and orbiting, waiting for the next group to create the next solution.

The industrial age may have created pyramid structures as a way of responding to the new efficiency of the assembly line. Today's complex workplace has no relationship to an assembly line or a pyramid.

John C. Maxwell's book, *The 21 Irrefutable Laws of Leadership,* has as its lead chapter, "The Law of the Lid." Maxwell describes a situation in which managers select managers whom they view as less than equal to their perceived talent. For example, a leader who sees him or herself as a seven will most likely hire people who are a six or below. Jim's selection of managers based on loyalty and not talent or leadership will be a problem. On the flip side, it is unlikely that a person who is greater than seven will want to work for Jim as he would offer little in their personal growth. The result is a company that will suffer from mediocre leadership.

Professional sport franchises illustrate the "Law of the Lid" every year. Managers or coaches are fired and new leaders are hired with the thought they can elevate the leadership potential and help the team achieve its goal. Teams are looking for a nine or ten so the coaching staff will be at least an eight. Even talented teams suffer when the leadership is lacking. Look at the difference between the Los Angeles Lakers in 1999 versus 2000. It is the same team with a different coach, Phil Jackson. He was hired because he was a leader in the sport of basketball coaching. He can lead talented teams and keep them focused on the goal of winning championships. Perhaps, if Sparky Anderson's theory is correct, Jackson would be a failure as a coach if not for Michael Jordan and the great Chicago Bulls teams of the 1980s. After two consecutive NBA championships Phil Jackson is the smartest coach in professional basketball.

COACH'S CHALKBOARD

Of the many reasons that may lead to Jim's job loss, the Law of the Lid will stand out. Jim could have been a great mentor for Rachel. He had no reason to be hostile; upper management had confidence in his ability and wanted him to take this role as mentor. His development of Rachel would have been seen as the best example of team player and he would have been a model for future star performers.

Jim's undermining of Rachel is reminiscent of the Watergate scandal of the 1970s. Nixon was going to be re-elected by a large margin of votes. Concern over the opposition was not justified and any action toward a clandestine operation yields little benefit and great risk. In hindsight, everyone now knows how stupid those decisions were and acknowledges that the risk was greater than the benefit. It cost Nixon his presidency.

Jim was faced with the same choice: undermining Rachel or supporting transformation. Supporting her would have solidified his political position and prevented the split camp. Both people become winners.

The split camp will lead to a coup. The high turnover rate will not be tolerated. The workforce will grow weary of seeing their friends hurt. The managers will tire of being labeled as winners or losers.

Jim will eventually move on to a new company. The remaining question is "how much damage has he caused?"

Strive to Instill Pride and Caring

As stated in the Introduction, it is amazing how graduates from colleges and universities are brimming with pride and loyalty to their school years after graduation. They buy school shirts and lamps, attend campus functions, donate to the alumni fund, and encourage their children to attend the same school. Some people swear that if they get cut on the hand they would bleed the school colors!

Colleges and universities go to great lengths to build pride and loyalty. Much of the graduate's commitment comes from learning and obtaining a degree that leads to a job. It is also a result of quality educators that act as mentors for young people. Other factors include physical and social activities like sporting events, dances, and possibly meeting a future spouse. Memories are created, and even though the homework is hard and sometimes has no applicability to the future, the student remembers the positive. Attending school was magical for almost everyone.

So where's the magic in the workplace? Does it end because dress codes force people to become something different? Is it because people are no longer students and they are told to grow up (i.e. corporate culture)? Why do people shrug or answer in short sentences about their job (while the same question about school will elicit a dissertation)? Perhaps the answer to these questions is that these people no longer have an identity.

Managers need to handle human resources like they are precious metals. Every person represents an investment that can someday pay back dividends (hence the term, human resource). Yet, when people quit, they leave because of a manager, not the company. The new millennium manger may need to earn a bonus on his or her ability to retain people over the long term. Indeed, many customer service centers have set a goal of less than 10 percent turnover per year.

Schools get students involved from the first day. They assign upper classman to guide freshmen through the first week and campus tours. Fraternities and sororities vie for new members; the athletic department looks for walk-ons to fill out their rosters. The school bookstore sells trinkets and other items giving freshman a sense of belonging. School functions include the dean, college presidents, and faculty members in an attempt to shorten the distance between the student and the college staff.

Businesses can respond by having mentors and coaches; CEOs and administrative leadership meet people one-on-one in company sponsored social settings and by distributing shirts, mugs, notebooks, and other paraphernalia build company identity. If a company is growing, it is important not to let the person feel unattended. If a university with over fifty thousand students can figure out how to welcome people, why can't a company with one thousand or ten thousand employees? Answer: it has to become a priority.

Once people sense they are the company's priority, they will respond by assuming responsibility. A company that cultivates a family atmosphere of "working hard and playing hard" has to be certain the entire management team understands the objective. The management team has to accept the philosophy is constant, not just at the company picnic.

For a globe concept to develop, "freshman" employees are shown how to navigate to various managers or departments. Any manager, who states they are too busy to help someone be successful, is just too busy (i.e. they didn't get the corporate message). Doors are open because the person in the doorway is a leader, a person whose brainpower will ignite the next round of growth.

Will the new work environment be more chaotic, noisy, and harder to manage? Absolutely, because innovation is noisy. In many schools today state-of-the-art computer labs are going underutilized. The main reason is computer learning allows students to accelerate at their own pace. Having students all over the place in teaching modules is just too chaotic for most traditional classroom teachers. Plus students tend to be noisy when they are excited about learning (keyboards pounding, mice clicking, feet tapping the floor to imaginary music). The room is energized and it can intimidate. Instead, the lab is used for study hall, where the good kids can go and surf the net for an hour.

The workplace will experience energy and positional managers will experience intimidation just as the out-of-touch teacher. Just as schools should not dismantle their computer labs because the right teacher doesn't exist today, companies should abandon the thought that it is too hard to find a better way. The right teacher may be hired next year. The next number one company in may be yours.

COACH'S CHALKBOARD

When a company recruits, interviews, and hires a person, a contract agreement is made. The company, in an effort to meet its needs, wants employees to:

• Work forty-hour weeks and/or a minimum of an eight-hour workday.
• Practice promptness and adherence to schedules and avoid workplace disruptions.
• Be committed to the workplace and provide the best results.
• Offer due respect to appropriate people.
• Provide the talents necessary to grasp the job and implement the tasks while exceeding the set standards.

In return, the company provides an hourly wage, benefits, training, and a safe work environment. This is the essence of the initial contract.

The contract gets refined when the employee attends orientation and training. Company-wide orientation usually discusses benefit packages and company perks and balances the good against what might get a person terminated (sexual harassment, stealing).

Training then focuses on the products and support resources that each person is expected to learn. Even if all the training is not completed, an agreement between the instructor and student is reached as to what will be added in the future. The contract is now complete. The company's perceptions and the employee's perceptions about the contract contents need to be in synchronization.

Trouble and dissent begins when, in the employee's eyes, the contract terms are violated. Employees are sensitive to fairness issues and whether proposed changes are going to be fair to them. The changes in question revolve around managerial decisions about how employees spend their time. Written laws or labor standards are not violated. It is the employee that feels violated.

Managers, under pressure to build growth, sometimes forget business' golden rule: employees are customers too. If a manager adds this idea to his or her philosophy inventory, changes will be made when unilateral input and a negotiated agreement are made.

Companies have the right and the need to change the way they do business. Usually, companies conduct focus groups to send up a test balloon for their proposed changes. If the test balloon passes the focus group muster, it is rolled out on a larger scale. Customers are notified and offered a chance to discontinue their relationship with the company or accept the new terms. If the customer drops out within acceptable means, the company retains its new policy. Otherwise, the company may need to redesign its proposed changes.

Top-shelf companies treat changes in the workplace in a similar manner. Meetings are held to discuss changes and solicit feedback. The feedback is reviewed and massaged into a new working model. A pilot group is formed and the objective and subjective evaluations are measured. If the proposed changes continue under scrutiny and are embraced by the pilot group, the new procedures are issued to everybody.

This model works when trust exists between management and the workforce. The strategy is not an idea that appears to be a bone thrown to the dog once in awhile so management feels they solicited input. For employee focus and pilot groups to work, they must be part of the support network.

Negotiations with the pilot group also need to be genuine. Writing new ideas, comments, and concerns that never appear again will shut down the process. Employees will spread the word that the process is bogus.

Companies and management always reserve the right to proceed ahead in the company's best interest. Future conflicts will be minimized if the workforce believes the company in its leadership, mission, and vision. Even if employee input has to be placed on reserve for the immediate future, the workplace will be satisfied if they are told the reasons why.

The golden rule is simple and bears repeating: employees are customers too. In this economy, it is difficult to find talented employees. Retaining talented people is not only fiscally sound, it is also necessary for survival of the company.

Top of the Ninth:
Avoiding Burnout By Creating Balance In Your Life

United States businesses lose billions of dollars every year in lost productivity as a result of employee fatigue. More importantly, a long-term study revealed that people who sleep less than six hours per night had a 70 percent higher death rate than those who slept seven to eight hours per night.

The cause of fatigue is a product of lifestyle choices. People feel rushed so they drink high doses of caffeine, smoke cigarettes, eat on the run (usually high fat and high salt foods), consume too much alcohol, eliminate productive activities such as exercise or reading, and fail to deal with stress. If you add jobs that are sedentary, anxiety provoking, and constantly changing, you may begin feeling like an over-filled balloon.

Sleep

The first part of your lifestyle plan is sleep and relaxation. Sleep and relaxation are not the same so taking a nap is not a form of relaxing. Relaxation includes reading, being entertained by some kind of media (music, movies, TV, audio books), meditation, gardening, and even your daily walks can be a form of relaxation. Relaxation is not a daily event but *multiple events daily*.

According to research at a leading university, lack of sleep leads to daytime drowsiness that produces decreased performance and reaction time. Sleep-deprived people actually experience short bursts of sleep where they will dose for seconds at a time without realizing what has happened.

Sleep needs to be productive, allowing your body to reach deep sleep, or REM. To maintain productive sleep, develop routines that the body learns to expect. Go to bed around the same time and get up every day around the same time. To illustrate how important routines are, speak to someone who works rotating shifts. Their ability to function decreases with every rotation. Initially, the person appears to function great, but over time their performance deteriorates. It is important to teach your body when to shut down and when to get started.

Studies indicate that people who do not practice sleep routines find themselves staying awake longer than they can afford and oversleeping the next day. Granted, you will have nights that you are not tired or will wake up too soon. Use this time for relaxation, carefully picking activities that will allow you to return to sleep. Physical activities will stimulate your body and you will be more likely to be tired later in the day. Instead, try a warm bath or light reading in a comfortable chair. Even a short nap will allow you to refresh and feel more rested than a night of fitful sleep.

Be careful not to make your bed your enemy. As strange as it may sound, many people who find themselves very tired go to bed and immediately wake up. Over time, they begin to treat the bed as an enemy, thinking that as soon as their head touches the pillow, they pop awake. If you do wake up, get out of bed and do something else. If you find your mind racing because the bedroom is quiet, create some productive noise like background music or nature sounds. Eventually, you can overcome this temporary bout of insomnia.

Naps are productive, but usually not practical. Few companies in the United States encourage their employees to take a nap around mid-shift. Because companies don't condone napping as productive does not mean it should only be reserved for young children. As people grow older, their ability to sleep is compromised; the best years for sleeping are between the ages of eleven and fourteen. Therefore, naps are a logical alternative to a full night of sleep. If you find yourself in a streak of poor productive sleep, attempt to schedule several nap times. A suggestion is to set aside twenty minutes, but take what you can get.

COACH'S CHALKBOARD
What Is Sleep Apnea?

Sleep apnea is a serious medical problem that can be life threatening. The term refers to a deprivation of oxygen during sleep. Sleep apnea is usually associated with snoring, or thick necks due to obesity, and affects both men and women. Typically, people with sleep apnea feel tired and sleepy throughout the next day because they cannot achieve deep sleep.

What usually happens when a person suffers with sleep apnea is the neck muscles relax, closing down the windpipe and creating an obstructed airway. This is more likely when the person has a large, fleshy neck, as the neck muscles are not able to support the additional weight, although weight is not always the problem. Snoring results when the soft tissues vibrate because of the air passing through a narrowing throat. Snorting or gasping when sleeping is a good indicator that the person may need to see an ear, nose, and throat doctor to determine the extent of passageway closure. The next step may be to see a pulmonary doctor, who may prescribe a sleep test where the person is monitored for at least one night.

So why does the person feel sleepy even though he or she spent seven or eight hours in bed? As the person relaxes and reaches a deeper state of sleep, the body relaxes. The airway passage narrows, lowering the amount of oxygen to the body. The initial defense mechanism is the snort or gasp, which startles the person to a more awakened state, and oxygen levels are restored. If the snort doesn't wake the person, the body will protect itself by tensing the muscles and awakening the person to a more conscious state thereby allowing more air through the passage. In either case, the person may be awakened by body defenses hundreds of times per night. Thus the person fails to reach deep sleep, and failure to have productive sleep leads to fatigue and sleepiness the next day. Over time, this deprivation of deep sleep creates a person who cannot concentrate and minimizes productivity. It also creates a dangerous potential of sleepiness on the roadway or while performing high-risk work tasks (like working around electricity).

A sleep test will require the person to spend a night in a sleep lab. The person will be monitored for oxygen saturation throughout the night. Brain waves will be recorded to determine the stages of sleep and the amount of peaceful sleep. If the diagnosis is sleep apnea, the alternatives may be behavioral changes such as losing weight and physical activity to strengthen the neck. A machine called the c-pap may also be used to fix the problem or a dental device can also be prescribed. Surgical intervention may be offered to reshape the inside of the throat by a laser to allow for more air passage. Finally, counseling may be offered that may include sleep positioning such as keeping the head higher than the chest.

For more information, visit the following Web sites. Seek medical help and discuss your options with a physician if you feel that you may have sleep apnea. He or she will recommend a specialist to be sure to rule out other related problems such as asthma or allergies.

www.webmd.com (use "sleep apnea" in search box; over 100 entries are available)

www.webmd.com/content/article/1680.51516 ("Tossing and Turning No More")

http://asda.org (American Academy of Sleep Medicine)

www.journal.sleep.org

www.drkoop.com (use "sleep apnea" in search)

www.myprimetime.com (sec sleep)

www.mayoclinic.com (use "sleep apnea" in search)

www.personalmd.com/index.html

www.ibionet.com (use alphabetical index, "S", and locate sleep disorders; provides online assessment forms)

http://medlineplus.gov/ (a service of National Library of Medicine)

Stress Reduction

To begin making changes, think about stress and how stress controls your day. Many times, a person starts the day in a rush by ignoring the alarm clock and then trying to catch up over the next hour. Sleeping past the first alarm or having trouble rising because of fatigue gets you off to a rough start. Stress creates a vicious cycle of uneasy rest, the need for more rest, and the feeling that you are never fresh.

And how does stress gain control over your life? It starts innocently enough when you take on added responsibilities like a job or raising children. This innocent start snowballs as more demands are made at work and at home. Then you feel like there should be more to life than just working or raising a family so you try to squeeze in a social life, thereby reducing free time on the weekends or evenings. Initially there seems to be a balance between work, home, and social life, but soon that balance is lost.

Workplace demands don't usually end at the close of the workday. Today, to have job success, it is necessary to take personal time to develop new skills and increase knowledge. Overtime work may be necessary to complete time-related tasks or to compensate for downsized departments. Upper management seems unreasonable, which at times creates uneasiness and lack of focus. This leaves you wondering about your competency, thereby challenging your confidence. Companies may promote the workaholic, forcing others to rethink how much time they devote to their family. Any of these potential scenarios affects your ability to manage stress and contributes to fatigue.

Once the work issues are put aside, then the family issues start. Children need nurturing, educational needs have to be addressed, and shopping for food and clothes has to be scheduled. Clothes and the house need to be cleaned and either the grass needs to be cut or the snow needs to be plowed. There are always tasks to finish at home. The completion of these tasks may take you well into the evening hours leaving you exhausted and looking at the clock to suddenly realize that it is midnight. Your time for exercise and relaxation has passed and now you must quickly wind down, fall asleep, and respond to the six o'clock alarm. You wake up, struggle to get out of bed, and immediately gather your wits so you can motivate the family to get going.

So goes the workweek in today's business world. The workweek may be any combination of days of the week and hours in a day. This schedule rotation is also a leading factor contributing to stress as people have a difficult time developing routines to help increase their efficiency at home and at play.

As a result of work, family, and social life, the first challenge is to create balance. Managing stress is the first step to creating balance. Notice the word *manage* and not the words *reducing* or *eliminating*. Stress will always exist because it is a perception of reality that an individual records in their mind. Stressful situations become reality when your mind makes it so.

People panic when activities begin to pile up. Perhaps because the person has no plan, which results in everything looking important. People who think through the day's needs have a plan and know what task needs to be done first. The activities themselves did not create the stress; it was the person through his or her reaction to the activities.

Perhaps this idea of perception sounds too simplistic to be believable. Consider this: unless you experienced a significant emotional event like a birth, death, birthday and so on, what happened to you last Tuesday? What happened to you last month on the 14th? Or, what happened to you last year on October 12th? You probably cannot recall specific details, but there's a good chance that on that particular day, there were several activities you deemed to be stressful. But, days, weeks, or months later, those activities are forgotten and you are dealing with a new set of activities that are causing you to react with stress. This is what is affectionately called "putting out fires." Fires are ongoing daily battles that distract people from quality outcomes and reduce success, thereby increasing stress.

And what about job-related activities that are stressful? Is it a lack of talent, knowledge, or skill that cause the stress, or is it your perception of what is needed? If lack of talent is the problem, get out and find a job that requires your talent. If knowledge or skill is the problem, get training to reduce those deficiencies.

If your job lacks direction or focus, your days will always be stressful. You don't know what to expect; therefore, you go in too many directions with no sense of accomplishment. You may need to weigh the alternatives and decide if your job is worth the stress you experience.

As individuals we sometimes forget that companies do not revolve around us. Companies were established before we started and they will survive after we leave. Our job is to define our workplace role and create positive outcomes. You can choose to become politically active to reach for new positions, or you can choose to be successful in your current position because your talents are matched suitably to the tasks. Just as you choose to become emotionally involved with your job, you can choose to be productive and a mentor. This is balance. Remember that it is not reality but your perception of reality that manages stress.

People and tasks can upset your stress management. You now accept that workdays can be poorly defined and wasteful. Therefore, work with your supervisor, manager or team members to plan activities in order of importance. Properly managed multiple tasks can be accomplished without creating uncontrolled stress.

Next, how do you address home life and the stress created by the family? As with work, when there are multiple needs for the family, it is important to decide what to attack first. What needs to be done, when does it need done, and is there anyone else who can do the task? Many years ago there was a television character named Edith Bunker. Edith would dote over her husband, Archie, and her family. Edith would literally run from room to room trying to meet the demands of the family. The other people were not handicapped. Edith never delegated any household chores to them and they were willing to be served at every turn.

It doesn't matter if you are male or female because today's parent roles make it tough for everyone. The point is to keep your perspective on what is important and let other family members play a role in everyday household needs.

In review, you are going to identify what you can control at work. If you cannot control it or it is not yours to control, let it go! Your manager or supervisor will encourage you to leave your personal problems at home. You also need to leave your work problems at work.

Next, sit down with your family and delegate work. Not only is it helpful to you, but it also helps develop necessary skills (like sewing and laundry) and responsibilities (taking care of the dog for example) in your children.

These changes will not occur overnight, but are a progression to a positive outcome. As a society, we all have access to many opportunities not afforded to people in less developed countries. These opportunities can be a great source of stress if not managed properly.

Another factor contributing to fatigue is people's access to entertainment and the Internet. Television has grown to twenty-four hours a day and hundreds of channels of entertainment. Premium channels and pay-per-view movies have led people to stay up longer on a work night than they originally intended. Even channels such as shopping networks capture the imagination of an audience and keep people addicted for too many hours. Lack of productive sleep affects our judgment and can lead to serious consequences such as injury or job loss. Lack of sleep will also negatively affect our ability to manage stress.

The Internet is now a major entertainment factor operating worldwide, uncensored, and with a base of over five hundred million sites to visit. Chat rooms, e-mail, music and video channels, and many other activities are causing adults to get less sleep and rest. You have probably read or heard about people who are now being treated for Internet addiction. As with many life choices, it is not the activity but the excessiveness of the activity that creates the problem.

If this scenario is not your problem, then skip ahead to the next paragraph. If you find television or the Internet is consuming large chunks of time, address this issue as you would any addictive behavior. First, find quality alternatives to the TV or computer and slowly implement them into your daily plan. For example, a brisk walk every evening instead of the world news program. Or, use your VCR to tape a variety of programs to watch later (or a different day) so you can manage your time better (just think about eliminating all those commercials!).

The problem is not TV or the computer; the problem is managing the time effectively. Only watch programs you really enjoy and skip over the other programs. Place a time limit for the computer and decide what entertainment value you want from each session.

Exercise

Exercise is the next lifestyle need to be addressed. Even though this choice is considered a positive, taking exercise to the extreme is not productive and can even lead to injury. To begin an exercise program, it is a good idea to see a doctor and get a physical. While you know you are fine, the physical can help define your physical limits (maximum target heart rate) that will allow your exercise program to be of quality value.

Exercise is synergistic, meaning that it adds up to greater benefits. You can walk in the morning for a short time and walk again in the afternoon to get your quality thirty to forty minutes. Other activities like gardening, yard work, dancing, and weight lifting are examples of activities that contribute to the overall fitness routine. Using low impact activities as the base for your program, it is possible (and recommended) to do something everyday. You will be impressed how fast your physical presence will improve, thereby changing your whole outlook and ability to manage stress. Your physical activity will burn calories and create a pleasant tiredness that leads to a productive night of sleep. This is the value of synergy: one plus one now equals four because the benefits are greater than the effort.

As you see from the preceding paragraph, it is not necessary to buy expensive workout equipment or join a workout club. An added benefit from the aforementioned activities is that other family members can be involved because anybody can do them and it is affordable. Soon, the entire family can see the activities as productive and all of you will be sleeping soundly throughout the night.

To review, when building a commitment to exercise, first see your doctor to help define the guidelines for a quality program. Next, see if you can plan time in the morning and evening hours to create a cumulative program that will take advantage of a variety of activities. Finally, do not overdo the activities because soreness can be a factor. Soreness prematurely stops many people from continuing their program (the "weekend war-rior" syndrome). Start slowly and under control, limit-ing your exposure to injury and increasing the potential for success.

Nutrition

Next address your diet and nutritional needs. Amer-ica has an abundance of food; recent grain harvests are so productive that thousands of tons of grain will rot before they can be used. The problem in America is that despite access to every imaginable type of food, people choose convenience. Thinking back to the earlier dis-cussion of pressure to do more in less time, conven-ience makes sense. Unfortunately, convenience foods are heavily laden with fats and empty calories that do not support an active lifestyle. Foods heavy with fat lead to people heavy with fat.

Many foods and desserts taste good. The problem becomes one of metabolic reaction. Flooding your body with an overabundance of calories causes the blood-stream to become laden with sugar. The pancreas at-tempts to maintain balance by releasing additional insu-lin to bond to the sugar and use the source as energy. The insulin falls behind in its work, opening the door for another metabolic action to occur, the storage of sugar energy as fat energy. Meanwhile the pancreas is still pumping out insulin to meet the original need. Now the excess sugar has been stored and there is too much insulin in the blood.

A diabetic knows that too much insulin causes fatigue (sometimes to the point where it can be life threatening for a diabetic). Too many calories have created a double whammy: fatigue and the creation of fat cells!

Food throughout the workday should be treated as a supplement, not a main course. To stay sharp at work, eat less at work. To prevent loss of energy, have healthy alternatives such as fruits, pretzels, crackers, or energy bars. Drink plenty of water because your body will be burning calories to create energy. The water aids the bloodstream to carry the nutrients throughout the body, thereby maintaining balance. To keep your brain functioning at its maximum, eat carbohydrates because the brain uses this food source for its energy supply.

The brain cannot use fatty foods until the body converts that energy into sugar. You can increase your body's efficiency by eating foods in the basic carbohydrate group (fruits, vegetables, breads). Energy reaches the brain faster and you reduce your fatigue. Save your big meals for holidays.

In summary, people seem more tired today than people from other generations. This fatigue factor hurts the person, the company they work for, and places pressure on the family through stress. Success for overcoming fatigue begins with a plan, both personal and for work. Focus your energies on those parts of the plan that have the highest priority. Look to achieve balance every day by including time for family, work, meals, sleep, and, most importantly, yourself. The results will accumulate over time and next year you will still be busy, but you'll feel more successful.

Top of the Tenth
Extra Innings

Leadership is about navigating an organization through calm and rough times. Here is a suggested list that every manager needs to consider as he or she begins to strive for excellence:

1. Define your plan, based on your company's stated goals. Everyone in your organization needs to know what it is going to take to make or keep the company successful. No details are too sensitive. In fact, the more sensitive the information shared, the more trust you show your workforce and the more they will respond.

2. Construct a timeline for the plan and use benchmarks to measure success. People do not respond to open-ended plans; they like to see closure.

3. Based on the timeline, design measurable objectives that will create roles for the workforce. As these objectives are reached, take time to celebrate. If an objective is not reached, hold team meetings to discuss what happened and what was learned from the experience. Placing blame is irrelevant; discovery and learning are essential.

4. Know your workforce and what motivates them individually. The word "me" is in team! You will not compromise teamwork by respecting the individual. In fact, the team will be stronger as each role is defined and molded to produce maximum results.

5. Set individual objectives that build on the plan's global objectives. Monitor progress at least twice a month and provide timely feedback to the person with respect to how well he or she is meeting the objective(s). Waiting to do a yearly review is meaningless.

6. If possible, consider whether objective(s) cross over to allow as many people as possible to have involvement in the workplace global objectives. People need to see the final product to appreciate quality outcomes. If you cannot provide the real world conclusion, provide simulation of the outcome(s).

7. Get feedback from every employee on a weekly basis. You will learn at least three new ideas per week

from *each person*! If you have a workforce of just ten people, you will gather a minimum of thirty ideas a week or over 1500 ideas a year. Given the statistical probability provided by a normal curve, at least 5 percent of ideas will be top quality. That means you will have seventy-five quality ideas per year. With a little refinement, you will get another 150 ideas that can be implemented. Human capital is your life force for a successful future.

8. Design incentives, including continuing education, to keep your best employees from leaving. Turnover is more than just a financial penalty. You could lose the cornerstone for your employee's morale and motivation.

9. Your employees are not clairvoyant! If you do not communicate with them, they will not respond in the direction you want them to head. Don't ask them to be creative and then be critical of the outcomes ("constructive criticism": what an oxymoron.). Use coaching to guide them through the creative process.

10. Finally, stand up for your employees. It is never easy to feel the wrath of an upper management individual who does not understand your leadership style. It will be real tempting to place blame on persons or technology for failure to reach a goal. Be prepared to discuss how the objective failed and

what you are doing to improve outcomes during the next benchmark period. Be sure to get upper management's "buy-in" for the updated plan.

If managing were easy, there would be no job category for manager. You stand in the worst possible position. Managers are the insulation in the hierarchical pyramid; they are the ones sacrificed when the team fails. And, everyone has his or her chance at failure; it is the bridgework to success. With this in mind, take your best shot at being a leader.

Top Of The Eleventh

Profit is not a process. Profit results from a well-executed plan. The purpose of a quality-oriented work environment is to create customer satisfaction. The process that leads to profit is the selection, development, involvement, and retention of talented employees. The ten-point summary is for managers who believe excellence is the norm.

One: Have A Plan

Even if your job is to drive Miss Daisy to the Piggly Wiggly, you need a plan. The route you will take under normal conditions and an alternate plan because of construction, traffic jams, or sudden storms. You know the goal and you know the routes that will take you there. Miss Daisy has confidence in you because you planned a route, carried it out, and were successful. Not once, but over and over again, you were successful. As Yogi

Berra would say: "If you don't know where you are going, you'll end up someplace else."

A plan charts a course and enables you to measure success. A plan allows for minor "fine tuning" that limits turmoil and keeps the workplace from "wild swings" of emotion. A plan builds momentum and maintains it through navigation. It is much easier to steer a ship once it is moving than when it is motionless.

The plan uses a company's mission to keep its focus. Turbulence is to be expected; you are not a sailor until you have navigated through rough water! A lower primate can manage a workplace when times are prosperous and people are efficient and competent.

The plan gets its energy from the company's vision. The workplace is a series of peaks and valleys. The roller coaster effect can discourage people, because the lows seem too long and the highs are too short. It takes an experienced manager to guide people through the daily grind and coach them to expect success. The best managers coach people not to get too high or too low. When things go well, enjoy the moment. When things are sour, expect better days ahead. A plan allows the manager to coach the simplified philosophy because he or she can show people the past progress and the future rewards. The manager's confidence is a role model for others.

Identify the talents and traits of those employees who provide the best customer satisfaction. Discover what makes them effective for achieving quality outcomes. Start matching people to the call center objectives rather than filling slots on a roster.

Once you have defined job talents, identify the necessary skills and knowledge each person will need. This list comes from the plan. Without a shopping list, it is difficult to pick the right people, offer the right training, or measure effectiveness. Coaching and mentoring become "chat sessions" instead of learning tools.

The plan you develop is not a single person effort. Have input from everyone as to how the work environment will develop its route to excellence. Everyone needs to agree that the vision is his or hers and the mission is meaningful.

The plan will not be a linear document that has checkmarks. To complement the structured efforts, the plan will have free-flowing elements. The outcomes will always support the vision. Some free-flowing ideas may stall or fail. This will happen in a creative environment. Help the team learn from the failure and encourage them to continue pursuing answers. At least the failure eliminated one idea that is not going to work at this time.

Two: Identify Barriers to Success

With the diversity existing in today's workplace, it is the manager's role to be a catalyst, a politician, and a defender. As a catalyst, the manager takes a person and a problem and creates an interaction leading to a positive outcome.

As a politician, it is the manager who sells the environment and the employees to upper management who may question the logic. The manager negotiates the tools and facilities necessary to keep the employees successful. The manager sells ideas by networking to gain the votes necessary to make changes. The manager serves as the sensory input to those who supply the budget (the eyes and the ears of upper management).

Taking calls in today's service center environment is a complex task. The number of calls coming into a center may decrease, but the time on each call will increase due to the complexity of maintaining customer satisfaction. Most consumer electronics work as expected and 95 percent of the customers will not need a service center. For those that have problems, providing necessary service can be a nightmare. Most consumer goods are made to be disposable in several years. Troubleshooting is a difficult task and has a limited number of steps to correct the problem. When these steps fail, it will be the talented service representative who keeps the customer satisfied as they pack the merchandise to return it to the factory for repairs.

It is the manager's responsibility to keep the service representatives' tools simplified. Inefficient software cannot consume the consultant's time. Tedious paperwork cannot consume the consultant's time. Rules and procedures that do not support customer satisfaction cannot consume the consultant's time. The environment needs to be kept clean from frivolous and nonproductive ideas. The manager must keep the environment simplified, not simple.

The manager keeps the consultant focused on the customer. The computer was supposed to be the slave for the workplace, not the other way around. Remember the process generates profit.

Three: Train for Success

The orientation program has a limited time frame and focuses on knowledge and skills. The orientation program also has limited value. Labor statistics suggest that the people available to staff service call centers are going to have limited work and educational experiences. In adult education, people will apply learning once they realize the need. Hence, the orientation program needs to be a combination of knowledge, skills, and application.

The orientation program goal is to build confidence. Activities and support materials give people confidence to complete the call center objectives.

Consistency between the training room and the work environment is essential. New employees cannot be exposed to one set of ideas in the training room and a second set in the workplace. Choose mentors and coaches who subscribe to the company's mission and vision and are in concert with the trainer. If students receive mixed messages, what will the customers receive?

As a manager, it is important to be involved with the trainer(s) to be certain the materials reflect the work environment. If the structured chaos challenges the most talented of your consultants, imagine the impact it will have on the new employee. The trainers need to be sensitive to help people understand that the constant changes and flow of the workplace are normal. The trainers need your plan as much as you need your plan.

Training focuses on experiential learning. Today, not many people book learn. The more senses involved in learning (see, hear, feel), the better the chances for successful adaptation. Construct simulation training to replicate the behaviors you feel essential for excellence. Using a computer as an instructor allows the new student to take as many tries necessary to be successful. The learner determines the time frame; the subject matter is determined by gap analysis; and ongoing education is a combination of short learning modules and team meetings.

Learning is not a linear process. Like the improvements on problem solving explored in the work environment, learning will also have various time frames.

Once the new employee achieves the minimum acceptable level of expertise, he or she will begin working with their assigned mentor. The mentor is responsible for new employee's integration into the workplace. The mentor enhances knowledge and skills and helps the person discover his or her talents and strengths. The mentor demonstrates how and why the skills apply to customer satisfaction.

Coaches have the responsibility of continuing new employee development by discovering the person's motivations and what they can contribute to workplace objectives. Coaches also plan the new employee's educational needs and work improvement plans. These plans are then submitted to the manager who uses the information to complement membership on teams.

Mentors and coaches are proactive measurements for new employees. They help identify individual needs and help the manager develop teams, goals and objectives. They determine what combinations are necessary to create a winning atmosphere. Gone are the days of winners and losers.

Four: Keep People Involved

The essence of a learning environment is everyone is involved. Teaching is not just the responsibility of one person. Adding creative components to the organizational plan is not just the manager's role. The responsibility for quality outcomes is not just the "quality group." Sharing is the norm in a learning environment. Every person contributes as often as possible.

The support network development fosters creativity. It is important to develop creativity before it is needed. People need to feel free to use the network to get answers and support for their problems and for guidance.

The workplace not only has people dedicated for knowledge and skills development, but also employee assistance counselors. The service call center is a microcosm of our society. This means people who are substance abusers, abused by their spouse, going through divorce or death in the family, struggling to maintain a quality home life while working unorthodox shifts, and people who never had to deal with irate customers will be in the mix. The employee is as much a customer of your company as the person on the phone. As a manager, show you care and help your people maintain their emotional balance.

Keeping everyone involved is not a matter of assigning busy work. Tasks need to be meaningful. The employee working on the task must feel they have competence and confidence to achieve a quality outcome. Teams are constructed with people who share enthusiasm for the goals and who complement each other's strengths. Create and maintain feedback loops not as much for management's benefit, but for the workplace's benefit.

The team or individual success must be celebrated. This celebration includes upper management individuals who originally set forth the mission and vision the consultants implemented. Full recognition of the team's accomplishments is the fuel for the next line of success.

COACH'S CHALKBOARD
What is Meaningful Work?

Any decision made exclusively by the manager may be perceived as busy work or dumping. It may also threaten the employee, as he or she cannot finish the request because they lack knowledge, skills, or talent.

Two approaches a manager can try are:

1. Send out a project or work list that needs to be done and have employees bid on the job(s), or

2. Gather ideas for projects based on the employees' stated motivators and talents.

Either way, the job will be more palatable, accomplished without grumbling and in a timely fashion.

Five: Retain the Best By Creating Futures

Incentives motivating employees are not always measured in dollars. Recognition and praise motivate many people. Employee surveys from many sectors reveal that perks such as flexible scheduling, self-improvement classes, and a casual work atmosphere offer better motivation than financial rewards. Money always sounds like a great motivator, but the riches are fleeting. Long-term perks are better for reinforcing employee loyalty.

Offering classes as a perk improves a person's knowledge and skills. Companies are no longer in a position to offer life-long employment. The changing face of business is too rapid for companies to commit long-term. Companies that care will try to make their employees "bullet-proof" to downsizing by helping them become more marketable. A person's security is one of Maslow's basic human needs and a company that offers people a "security blanket" receives loyalty in return.

"Click and brick" companies are creating many jobs and there is concern about their lasting ability. Only one company that existed in the 19th-century Dow-Jones still exists today (Give up? It's General Electric). Offer your employees security by giving them the flexibility to survive turmoil.

Employee retention is also reflected by a company's innovative pay structure. A one-size fits all mentality for pay scales makes it difficult to keep the best people in your organization. Using a staircase of financial improvement will encourage people to stay in your workplace instead of leaving for fifty cents an hour more elsewhere. It also reduces the potential of the "Peter Principle;" where people seek promotions not because they will enjoy the position or because they are qualified, but because they want a few more cents per hour.

As part of the plan developed in point one, the financial staircase is also presented. The armed forces have always used a system that alerts soldiers what the pay scale will be at the next level. He or she will still be a soldier, but now their knowledge, skills, experience, and talents are appropriately compensated.

In a hierarchical organization, hourly or salary wages keep people in their place. Look at the difference at a company like Microsoft where one out of every ten workers is a millionaire. Depending on the stock value, it is either the first, second, or third richest company in the world. Microsoft management realized unprecedented growth and wealth, which would not have been possible with traditional methodology. So why do companies continue to cling to the industrial age with respect to positions, job descriptions, and compensation? Perhaps that is why hundreds of companies disappear yearly.

Six: Use Leadership, Not Control, to Stimulate Responsibility

Positional leadership is found in grand titles (Regional General Manager, Northeast United States, North America, Earth). Positional leaders do their best to legislate responsibility (sometimes using fear), monitor numerous quantitative measurements tied to financial incentives, and manage a host of middle management whose job is to police the work environment. Employees respond using passive resistance and demonstrating an "it's just a job" attitude. Dilbert cartoons depict these business attitudes. Employees see their own situations in the cartoons, making this strip one of the most popular.

Leaders know that you fine-tune a racing car, not govern the speedometer. Any fine racing machine needs wide-open spaces for full throttle excitement.

If customer-centered quality outcomes are not the goal, then hire anyone to run and work in the environment. If quality is the goal, find leaders, plan and measure carefully, train to the maximum, identify talents, then stand back and open the throttle.

Trust is the cornerstone to superior leadership. Trust is not an earned token. When a company hires an individual, trust is part of the package. Any manager who operates by asking people to earn his or her trust doesn't trust people. Since trust is not an incrementally earned trait, the leader sends a message that people can't be trusted, so keep an eye on them.

Leaders need to adapt a position Peter Senge refers to as "open and broad." Be prepared to change yourself to fit the need of the workplace and the employees. The adage of "my way or the highway" is an old movie cliché. Today's workforce responds to managers who look for participation in problem solving and refuse to categorize solutions within a black or white philosophy.

Leaders never stop learning. The beauty of learning after you finish school is that you learn to fill your needs. It is no longer necessary to learn for the purposes of regurgitating answers to satisfy an instructor's tenure. Learning is meaningful and will be applied to your workplace needs.

COACH'S CHALKBOARD
Timing is Critical for Success

The problem with storing ideas or creating long-term folders is that managers use that information as employee feedback months after the fact. These items may turn up on sheets of paper in an employee's file and will ultimately be used for the annual performance evaluation. These items tend be negative comments or concerns about the employee and may not be objective.

The business world's greatest oxymoron is the term "constructive criticism." Criticism is rarely constructive. A plan to address the employee's perceived needs is constructive. Being critical lacks respect for employees and will create turnover.

Instead of this traditional look at annual reviews, why not discuss items as they occur? "Just in time" type of feedback not only alerts the employee that something is amiss but also alerts the manager to small problems. A top-shelf company that says "here's the goal, now go get it" will have employees miss the pathway or get lost on the path. These are not fatal mistakes unless the issue goes unattended for months at a time.

If you are training a new puppy and leave the house for several hours to take care of some business, the puppy may also take care of some business on your carpeting. Some people will come home after several hours, see the mess and begin scolding the puppy (maybe even rubbing their nose in the spot). Now puppies do not have a sense of time or reasoning. Scolding is counter-productive with the puppy. After all, urine is used to mark their territory and if a person rubs the nose in the spot, the puppy may think that the behavior should be repeated.

Employees should be much better equipped to handle situations that happen within several hours. They should also be able to explain the reasons behind their decision. The manager who senses the need for intervention may uncover a good idea that will enhance the workplace. Simply documenting an event for future discussions may lead to clouded memories and a situation where learning opportunities are missed because of poor timing.

Seven: Show People You Care
It is easy for employees to become complacent. The daily workday routines consume as much as 50 percent

of their time. Toss in sleep, daily living activities, meals, and other family needs, the average person has less than one hour of personal time, five days a week. In addition, the days off become cram sessions to catch up or get ahead.

The results of this brutal seven-day week is to relegate work as a place to relax, socialize, and do enough work to keep the "floor police" at bay. In hierarchical organizations, managers, supervisors, and team leaders are hired and trained to minimize complacency. Fear, criticism, and de-incentives are used to coerce increased productivity.

This should not shock anyone as our society has responded this way for decades. Our culture asks people for the right answers or you get negative feedback. The best managers are the ones who deliver the negative feedback without alienating the employee. He or she makes the person feel good as they criticize the individual for not being clairvoyant and anticipating the right outcomes.

Genuine caring is not about fair disciplinary actions or tough love. This is an adult world in the service call center and people expect respect, not patronizing feel good talks. Caring is knowing the people in the workplace, their hopes and dreams, their motivations, fears, and what they expect and need from you. Caring is the proverbial two-way street: you get what you give.

Once a person adopts a caring attitude, the responsibility of avoiding complacency will follow. As a manager, you will not need to devote valuable resources to enforce quantitative measurements. Instead, the disciplinarians can now be teachers, coaches, and mentors.

Caring is honesty and giving people feedback about their work based on predetermined objectives. Timely feedback constructed around the organization's needs allows employees to build appropriate skills to reach quality outcomes. Feedback is not about past weaknesses, but future contributions. Does this sound like something addressed once a year in a performance appraisal? Is it necessary to find fault with people in order to get them to work harder?

Eight: Leaders Are Politicians Negotiating Winning and Success for Both Sides

An excellent leader does not seek credit or glory. People will follow an excellent leader anywhere. Good leaders are idolized and their reputation precedes them. Remember any leaders you are fond of from the past or present and study why that person has legions of followers. The successful leader has an immediate goal to make everyone around them as successful as they want to become. The leader is the negotiator creating win-win scenarios.

The idea of creating a winners and losers environment is self-defeating. What purpose does it serve a manager to know that as many as 75 percent of his or her workers are a failure? If the goal is to build confidence and competence, what has been achieved having even one person labeled as a loser? Every person is spending at least 35 percent of his or her awake hours in the service call center. Little opportunity exists for a person to be successful outside of work to balance the loser tag your environment brands on them. Unkind and unjustified branding demoralizes and lowers self-esteem. It is tough to make excellence the norm when people don't feel competent.

If a person is incompetent, then be fair and terminate that person. Harassment and discrimination lawsuits are the result of managers and corporations who don't work with an employee. Not everyone will fit your objectives or contribute to excellence. These people represent your company to your customers. You are better off without them, but do the next step legitimately. Base decisions on performance measurements and failure to achieve work plan objectives despite continuing education. Offer the person job counseling and show you care.

Once you have your core of talented people, work with recruiting to bring in more. Look for the "eights and nines" in leadership because they will help your work environment achieve new levels of progress. Decide what activities will make winners out of everybody and build those ideas into the workplace. Find roles for people to be successful in. It is not a sign of weakness to encourage people to admit the job is a poor fit and to try something else. Work environments have a multitude of needs that can utilize almost any talent.

The expansion or contraction of your workplace will be directly related to your courage. Outside your environment, negotiate with other managers to provide the tools necessary to help your people be more successful.

Negotiate with upper management to embrace the new environment and supply incentives and performance scales to keep employees. If truth and honesty are missing ingredients in your organization, be wary because you are also being lied to.

Nine: Be Creative and Innovative

Progress in a linear fashion worked well in the last century. Today's customer's expectations are mounting because they live in a "big promise" business and service world. Linear progression will cost companies their customers. Customers will seek innovators and service groups with a high level of responsiveness. Having a staff devoted to quality outcomes is necessary for survival. Customers will still respond to the human voice that is knowledgeable and caring.

Because the information and call complexity is growing faster than available talent, create response teams. These teams each own a component of the solution and together they become a better problem-solver than the parts. Involving these teams in creativity exercises will enhance their skills and build on their strengths.

Creativity activities are not hastily put together when the company senses trouble is afoot. Creativity is a skill that needs practice just like tennis or golf. Creativity is not a knee-jerk reflex discussed in a one-hour meeting. Hastily assembled ideas created a management team that feels the need to say something to avoid wearing the stupid tag will be the proverbial goose chase.

As part of the environment and network, schedule creativity classes to keep people sharp. Brainstorming is a learned technique requiring trust within the groups. People are less likely to contribute if their ideas are judged and challenged in front of their peers.

Innovation can occur from any source. This is the important concept of getting people involved. Today's manager cannot know what the employee or customer needs. He or she depends on feedback from the staff to help determine the next sequence of problem-solving events. Then assemble teams to test and evaluate the new solution to determine effectiveness. A manager will not get support and growth without a group that cares about their jobs.

Stimulate the workplace to get the corks out of the bottles. Create an atmosphere energized with the excitement of discovery. Consider the following: there are two hundred people and each person is asked to generate 15 to 25 ideas or more. This will yield around 450 new ideas. Approximately 5 percent of those ideas (twenty) are "restaurant quality" and need little polishing. Another 10 percent will need teams to develop into a polished idea. By the end of three months, you now have 65 new ideas being implemented or evaluated. You may have one hundred ideas that could be supported by the advancement of the original 65 ideas. Now, synergy has been established and the workplace will no longer wait for one person to come up with a good idea.

Ten: Introduce New Skills Often

Stress management, problem solving, financial planning, health and wellness and listening techniques are skills that enhance people both on and off the job. Regularly scheduled programs, even on the employees' own time, demonstrate the company commitment to the employee. Connecting people with outside vendors who can offer continuing education credits will also increase a person's commitment to the company.

Much of the effort a company receives from its employees is directly related to how people see themselves. A positive self-esteem is conveyed to customers and customers sense the employee's attitude (just like the study that showed customers could detect a dissatisfied employee). Developing a positive self-esteem is not a lecture and a couple of slides. Remember the resource pool demographics that the person is representing. Building self-esteem will be an on-going commitment by the company to the employee.

Call center jobs are sedentary and perfect for developing three side effects: overweight, out-of-shape, and stressed representatives. It is unlikely that people know anything about lifestyle changes other than what they read in popular supermarket magazines. Teach people how to choose what they eat and stress that how much they exercise is related to controlling stress and having more success as an individual. People will eat fast food for lunch or dinner only to find they require a nap when they finish. A nap is not possible, so they are forced to struggle through the hour or so until their energy returns. That hour can be the busiest part of a workplace day and you just had forty to sixty calls answered by people feeling pretty dull.

Physical fitness is important on any job. Again, people talk about getting started but do not have any quality information to guide them. Instead, they buy in-home equipment, overwork on the first day, and suffer from soreness for the next week. So much for the in-house exercise program and the thought of getting in shape. A recent study suggested a person should walk five thousand steps daily to maintain fitness. This translates to five miles of walking and would include time spent walking around the workplace. Less than 3 percent of the people studied covered that much area walking daily. Exercise is not magical or difficult to start. The problem is getting started and staying dedicated. Companies offering fitness programs thought the effort might reduce insurance claims by minimizing chronic illness. The best benefits came from the increased productivity, camaraderie, and commitment to the company.

Stress reduction is more than closing one's eyes and visualizing a happy place. Stress is environmental and self-induced. Divorce rates in the United States are approaching 50 percent, so it is easy to appreciate how difficult it is for people to be together. In the workplace, personality clashes, broken relationships, and other interpersonal relationships can wreak havoc on a manager's best-laid plans. It is a great source of stress that can affect many people (they may take sides, for example). It is important for your employee assistance person to mange turmoil.

Self-induced stress includes such lifestyle choices as smoking cigarettes (and other substances), alcohol abuse, drug abuse, caffeine addiction, and lack of sleep. Any lifestyle affected by substance abuse will require outside help. Fatigue is a major contributor to productivity loss. In fact, injuries and deaths attributed to lack of sleep cost companies billions of dollars yearly. People have been observed falling into micro sleep, a condition triggered by fatigue where the person doses off for several seconds and recovers without realizing what happened.

Many suggestions have been made for enticing employees to stay, improve, and help recruit talented people to work for your company. Whatever steps may be taken next, just remember, you are taking steps. Changing an organization is a journey and has no endpoint. Do something small involving a fraction of the workforce. Allow people to sell the ideas to others and then begin increasing the number of teams and personnel involvement. Eventually you will get the ship moving in the right direction.

Index

Suggested Reading

The 7 Habits of Highly Effective People, Stephen Covey, Simon and Schuster, 1989

The 21 Irrefutable Laws of Leadership, John Maxwell, Thomas Nelson Publishers, 1998

99% Inspiration: Tips, Tales and Techniques for Liberating Your Business Creativity, Bryan Mattimore, American Management Association, 1994

A Better Place to Work: New Sense of Motivation Leading to High Productivity, Adolf Haasen and Gordon Shea, American Management Association, 1997

The Abilene Paradox, Jerry Harvey, Lexington Books, 1998

Advanced Selling Strategies, Brian Tracy, Simon and Schuster, 1996

Age Wave, Ken Dychtwald, Ph.D., St. Martin's Press, 1989

Are Your Lights On? How to Figure Out What the Problem Really Is, Gerald Weinberg, Dorset House Publishing, 1990

Beyond Race and Gender: Managing Diversity in the Workplace, R. Roosevelt Thomas, Jr., American Management Association, 1991

Bringing Out the Best in People, Alan Loy McGinnis, Augsburg Publishing House, 1985

Building Learning Communities in Cyberspace, Rena Palloff and Keith Pratt, Jossey-Bass, Inc., 1999

Building the High Performance Sales Force, Joe Petrone, American Management Association, 1994

Call Center Magazine, www.callcentermagazine.com (USA subscription: 888-824-9793)

Calling A Halt to Mindless Change: A Plan for Commonsense Management, John Macdonald, American Management Association, 1998

The CEO Paradox, Thomas Horton, American Management Association, 1992

The Change Masters, Rosabeth Moss Kanter, Simon and Schuster, Inc., 1983

The Change Monster, Jeanie Daniel Duck, Crown Publishing Group, 2001

CIO, www.cio.com (USA subscription: 800-788-4605)

Closing, A Process, Not A Problem, Virden Thornton, Crisp Publications, Inc., 1995

Closing Techniques That Really Work, Stephen Schiffman, Adams Media Corporation, 1994

Coaching for Commitment: Interpersonal Strategies for Obtaining Superior Performance from Individuals and Teams, Dennis Kinlaw, Jossey-Bass, 1999

Coaching for Development: Skills for Managers and Team Leaders, Marianne Minor, M.S.W., Crisp Publications, Inc., 1995

Coach Yourself to Success: 101 Tips From a Personal Coach for Reaching Your Goals at Work and in Life, Talane Miedaner, Contemporary Books, 2000

Competing on the Edge: Strategy vs Structured Chaos, Shona Brown and Kathleen Eisenhardt, Harvard Business School Press, 1998

Contemporary Issues in Leadership, William Rosenbach and Robert Taylor, Westview Press, Inc., 1989

Control Your Destiny or Someone Else Will, Noel Tichy and Stratford Sherman, Harper Business, 1994

Creating the Virtual Classroom: Distance Learning with the Internet, Lynette Porter, John Wiley and Sons, Inc., 1997

Customers.com, Patricia Seybold, Random House, 1998

Customer Focused Selling, Michael Bosworth, McGraw-Hill, 1995

The Dance of Change: The Challenge of Sustaining Momentum in Learning Organizations, Peter Senge, et al., Doubleday, 1999

Danger in the Comfort Zone, Judith Bardwick, American Management Association, 1991

Deep Change, Robert Quinn, Jossey-Bass, Inc., 1996

Dinosaur Brains, Albert Bernstein and Sydney Craft Rozen, John Wiley and Sons, 1989

Empires of the Mind, Denis Waitly, William Morrow and Company, Inc., 1995

The Encouragement Book: Becoming a Positive Person, Don Dinkmeyer and Lewis Losoncy, Prentice Hall, Inc., 1980

Enterprise One to One: Tools for Competing in the Interactive Age, Don Peppers and Martha Rogers, Doubleday, 1997

Fast Company, www.fastcompany.com (USA subscription: 800-542-6029)

Fatal Illusions: Shedding 12 Unrealities That Can Keep Your Organization from Success, James Lucas, American Management Association, 1997

The Fifth Discipline Fieldbook, Peter Senge, et al., Random House, 1999

First, Break All The Rules, Marcus Buckingham and Curt Coffman, Simon and Schuster, 1999

First Things First, Stephen Covey, Simon and Schuster, Inc., 1994

Four Levers of Corporate Change, Peter Brill and Richard Worth, American Management Association, 1997

Future Edge: Discovering the New Paradigms of Success, Joel Barker, William Morrow and Company, Inc., 1992

Game Plan, Bob Buford, Zondervan Publishing House, 1997

Getting Employees to Fall in Love with Your Company, Jim Harris, Ph.D., American Management Association, 1996

Getting Together: Building Relationships As We Negotiate, Roger Fisher and Scott Brown, Penguin Books, 1988

Getting Past No: Negotiating with Difficult People, William Ury, Bantam Books, 1991

Gung Ho! Ken Blanchard and Sheldon Bowles, William Morrow and Company, Inc., 1998

How to Manage Conflict: A Practical Guide to Effective Conflict Management, William Hendricks, Ph.D., National Press Publications, 1991

How to Think Like Leonardo da Vinci, Michael Gelb, Delacorte Press, 1998

High Value Manager, Florence Stone and Randi Sachs, American Management Association, 1995

The Innovator's Dilemma, Clayton Christensen, Harvard Business School Press, 1997

Knights of the Tele-Round Table, Jaclyn Kostner, Ph.D., Warner Books, 1994

Knock Your Socks Off Selling, Jeffrey Gitomer and Ron Zemke, American Management Association, 1999

Lead, Follow or Get Out of the Way, Jim Lundy, Avant Books, 1986

Lead Your Staff to Think Like Einstein, Create Like Da Vinci and Invent Like Edison, Don Blohowiak, Irwin Professional Publishing, 1995

Leadership by Design: How Benchmark Companies Sustain Success Through Investing in Continuous Learning, Albert Vicere and Robert Fulmer, Harvard Business School Press, 1997

Leading on the Creative Edge, Roger Firestien, Ph.D., Pinon Press, 1996

Leapfrogging the Competition: 5 Giant Steps to Becoming a Market Leader, Oren Harari, Ph.D., Prima Publishing, 1999

Life is an Attitude: Staying Positive During Tough Times, Elwood Chapman, Crisp Publications, Inc., 1992

Listening: the Forgotten Skill, Madelyn Burley-Allen, John Wiley and Sons, Inc., 1996

Management Challenges for the 21st Century, Peter Drucker, Harper Business, 1999

The Management Compass: Steering the Corporation Using Hoshin Planning, American Management Association, 1995

Management of Stress, David Frew, Nelson Hall, 1977

Management Review, www.amanet.org (published online)

Mentoring, Gordon Shea, Crisp Publications, Inc., 1997

Motivating People to Care, Bernard Hugh Petrina, Renewal Resources, 1989

Neanderthals at Work, Albert Bernstein and Sydney Craft Rozen, John Wiley and Sons, Inc., 1992

The New Pioneers, Thomas Petzinger, Jr., Simon and Schuster, 1999

The New Realities, Peter Drucker, Harper and Row, 1989

Next: Trends for the Near Future, Ira Matathia and Marian Salzman, The Overlook Press, 1999

Northbound Train, Karl Albrecht, American Management Association, 1994

Now, Discover Your Strengths, Marcus Buckingham and Donald Clifton, Ph.D., Simon and Schuster, 2001

One to One Future: Building Relationships One Customer at a Time, Don Peppers and Martha Rogers, Doubleday, 1993

The Online Teaching Guide, Ken White and Bob Weight, Allyn and Bacon, 2000

Outrageous: Unforgettable Service and Guilt-Free Selling, T. Scott Gross, American Management Association, 1998

Positive Leadership, www.ragan.com (USA subscription: 800-878-5331)

The Power of Persuasion, G. Ray Funkhouser, Ph.D., Random House, Inc., 1986

Principle-Centered Leadership, Stephen Covey, Simon and Schuster, 1991

Pulling Together: The Power of Teamwork, John Murphy, Wynwood, 1997

Reaching the Peak Performance Zone: How to Motivate Yourself and Others to Excel, Gerald Kushel, American Management Association, 1994

Real Power: Business Lessons from the Tao Te Ching, James Autry and Stephen Mitchell, Riverhead Books, 1998

Results Based Leadership, Dave Ulrich, Jack Zenger, and Norm Smallwood, Harvard Business School Press, 1999

Rethinking the Corporation: Architecture of Change, Robert Tomasko, American Management Association, 1993

The Sales Bible, Jeffrey Gitomer, William Morrow and Company, Inc., 1994

The Salesman's Book of Wisdom, Dr. Criswell Freeman, Walnut Grove Press, 1998

Selling for People Who Hate to Sell, Brigid McGrath Massie, Prima Publishing, 1996

Selling Power, www.sellingpower.com, (USA subscription: 800-752-7355)

Semper Fi: Business Leadership the Marine Corps Way, Dan Carrison and Rod Walsh, American Management Association, 1999

Secrets of Effective Leadership, Fred A. Manske, Jr., Leadership Education and Development, Inc., 1990

The Six Imperatives of Marketing, Allan Magrath, American Management Association, 1992

Six Thinking Hats, Edward De Bono, Little, Brown and Co., 1999

Smart Leadership, Anthony Vlamis, American Management Association, 1999

Solution Selling, Michael Bosworth, McGraw-Hill, 1995

Success for Dummies, IDG Books Worldwide, Inc., 1998

The Success Factor, Sidney Lecker, M.D., RR Donnelley and Sons, Co., 1986

Taking Charge: Making the Right Choice, Perry Smith, Avery Publishing Group, Inc., 1988

The Tao of Pooh, Benjamin Hoff, Penguin Books, 1982

The Te of Piglet, Benjamin Hoff, Penguin Group, 1994

Team Built: Making Teamwork Work, Mark Sanborn, MasterMedia Limited, 1992

Territorial Games: Understanding and Ending Turf Wars at Work, Annette Simmons, American Management Association, 1998

The Thinker's Way, John Chaffee, Ph.D., Little, Brown and Company, 1998

The Time Trap, Alec Mackenzie, American Management Association, 1990

Tough Minded Leadership, Joe Batten, American Management Association, 1989

The Trainer's Toolkit, Cy Charney and Kathy Conway, American Management Association, 1998

Transforming the Way We Work: The Power of Collaborative Workplace, Edward Marshall, American Management Association, 1995

Virtual Learning, Roger Schank, McGraw-Hill, 1997

Vroom! Turbo Charged Team Building, Michael Shandler and Michael Egan, New Vision Technologies, Inc., 1996

Why Didn't I Think of That? Roger Firestien, United Educational Services, Inc., 1989

When Smart People Work for Dumb Bosses: How to Survive in a Crazy and Dysfunctional Workplace, William Lundin, Ph.D. and Kathleen Lundin, McGraw-Hill, 1998

When Sparks Fly: Igniting Creativity in Groups, Dorothy Leonard and Walter Swap, Harvard Business School Press, 1999

Winnie-the-Pooh on Management, Roger Allen, Penguin Group, 1994

Winning Manager, Julius Eitington, Gulf Publishing Company, 1997

The Winning Trainer, 3rd Edition, Julius Eitington, Gulf Publishing Company, 1996

Winning Ways, Dick Lyles, G.P. Putnam's Sons, 2000

Workforce Renewal, Bernard Hugh Petrina, Crisp Publications, Inc., 1994

Working Without A Net: How to Survive and Thrive in Today's High Risk Business World, Morris Shectman, Pocket Books, 1994

You Can Do it: How to Encourage Yourself, Lewis Losoncy, Prentice Hall, Inc., 1980

Zapp! In Education, William Byham, Ph.D., Development Dimensions International Publications, 1992

Zapp! The Lightening of Empowerment, William Byham, Ph.D., Ballantine Books, 1988

Acknowledgments

I would like to thank my editor Shannon Murdock for her valuable assistance and insights that lent support to the diligence necessary to complete this task. I would also like to thank my mentors and all the wonderful people that provided the creative inspiration found throughout the book.

About the Author

For the past twenty-five years, William V. Jones has been a manager, educator, coach, and mentor in healthcare, education, and telecommunications. He has aided hundreds of people in identifying their potential and achieving successful outcomes. He obtained a master's degree from the Pennsylvania State University and business and leadership training from Gannon University. He is a member of the American Management Association, the International Society for Performance Improvement, and the American Society of Training and Development.

As an author, Jones has written over a dozen publications ranging from specific healthcare treatment strategies to business plans. He has lectured throughout the United States and Canada, primarily on the topic of creating a successful work environment. Jones also teaches computer applications, Web design, and entrepreneurial strategies for local institutions.